IN THE DAYS OF WILLIAM
THE CONQUEROR

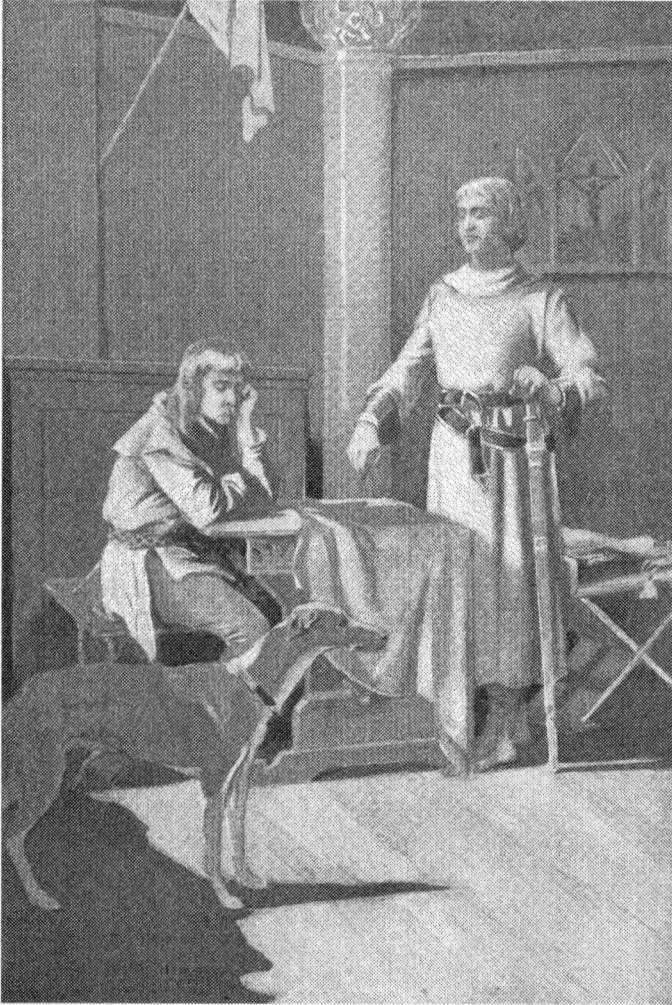

"WILL YOU PROMISE ME?"

IN THE DAYS

OF

WILLIAM THE CONQUEROR

BY

EVA MARCH TAPPAN, Ph.D.

ILLUSTRATED BY J. W. KENNEDY

YESTERDAY'S CLASSICS

CHAPEL HILL, NORTH CAROLINA

This edition, first published in 2006 by Yesterday's Classics, is an unabridged republication of the work originally published by Lee and Shepard in 1901. For a listing of the books published by Yesterday's Classics, please visit www.yesterdaysclassics.com. Yesterday's Classics is the publishing arm of the Baldwin Project which presents the complete text of dozens of classic books for children at www.mainlesson.com under the editorship of Lisa M. Ripperton and T. A. Roth.

ISBN-10: 1-59915-036-0
ISBN-13: 978-1-59915-036-9

Yesterday's Classics
PO Box 3418
Chapel Hill, NC 27515

To the Memory of
MY FATHER

PREFACE

THE story of William the Conqueror is the story of the man who for more than a quarter of a century was the most prominent personage of western Europe. Into whose hands shall England fall, was one of the two or three great questions of the time, and it was William who solved the problem.

Whether or not his claim to the English throne was just, the people and their new sovereign seemed made for each other. The English could follow; William could lead. The English could endure; William could strike the blow that made endurance needless. The English were inclined to be grave and serious; William enjoyed a jest. The English were a little slow in their thinking; William was quick-witted. The English would yield to fate; William was fate itself.

William's reign was a period of transition, and in such a time both faults and virtues stand out in bold relief. Whatever in the character of the Conqueror the twentieth century may find worthy of blame or of praise, no student of his life will deny that his faults were those of his time, that his virtues were his own.

EVA MARCH TAPPAN.

WORCESTER, MASSACHUSETTS,
November, 1900.

CONTENTS

CHAPTER I

THAT WHICH HE WOULD HAVE

"COME to the window, Ermenoldus. See how the country stretches out,—fields and vineyards and corn land! There's no richer ground in the whole duchy of Normandy."

"You and Duke Richard rule it together, do you not, my lord?"

"No. We hold it together after a fashion, but he rules. I am his vassal. Hiesmes is mine, and this goodly castle of Falaise ought to go with it."

"Was the duke your father's favorite, my lord?"

"Doesn't it look like it, when he left me only Hiesmes and then cut off the best part of it for Richard?"

"Could it have been suggested to him, my lord?"

"You mean, did Richard tell him to do it," said Count Robert bluntly. "Who knows what one man has said to another? Richard was with him from morning till night. My father called him a 'good youth.' I suppose I was a bad one," and the young man laughed

1

recklessly. "Anyway, Richard is Duke of Normandy, and I am only the Count of the Hiesmois; and here I am in the village of Falaise that ought to be mine, collecting taxes that ought to be mine, and putting them safely away for my brother in the treasure-room of the castle that ought to be mine."

"This castle seems to be of good strength, my lord. The walls are thick and heavy. It would not be easy to batter them down. It stands at the very edge of the cliff, and the cliff falls down sheer to the valley. No one could approach on that side."

"No; it's a strong castle, but I have none that could not be captured in a day. Come to the window again, Ermenoldus. See what a mass of rock the castle is built on, and how it juts out over the valley! Across the Ante is that other great, jagged precipice. You're a wizard, Ermenoldus; I verily believe you are. Couldn't you build me a castle on Mount Mirat yonder that would be as strong as this?"

I'm not enough of a wizard to give you a castle, my lord," said Ermenoldus; "and yet, there's more than one way," he half whispered. Count Robert did not hear the whisper, for he had turned again to the narrow window.

"If those girls are as pretty as they are graceful and merry," he said, "they would be well worth seeing. Ermenoldus, will you call some one to get my horse? or, if you stamp three times on the stone under your feet, won't the horse come of its own accord, all saddled and bridled?"

"You think too highly of the little that I have learned," said Ermenoldus.

"I'm not sure, though," said the count laughing, "but you are in league with the fiend himself and know all that there is to be known. Whence do you come and whither do you go? You appear and then you disappear, and all I know is that you are gone."

"Never did I go faster than you will go to gaze upon the pretty maidens washing linen on the banks of the stream," said Ermenoldus; "only I beg you, my lord, don't ride down over the cliff in your haste. All my magic could not save you then;" but Count Robert was already at the gate, and the next minute he was galloping down the rough, rocky way that led to the foot of the cliff.

The linen had been spread out on the grass to dry and to whiten in the hot sun, and the young girls were frolicking in the ripples of the little stream, laughing and splashing water at one another. One had bent down a green bough and held it in front of her face to protect it.

"By my faith!" said Count Robert to himself, "if that maiden's face is as fair as her little feet are white, she's prettier than all the high-born dames at my brother's castle." Just then the maiden let go the green branch and it sprang up above her head.

"Let's dance," she said, "not splash water at one another like children."

"That's a fairer face than I ever saw before," thought the count, as he stopped his horse, and hidden by the trees, gazed at the young girls in their playful imitation of the village dance, their white feet now twinkling in the green grass on the river's brink, and now splashing rainbow drops around them.

"See how high the sun is," said one of the girls. "The linen is dry, and we must go home."

"I'm tired. I'm going to rest awhile here under the trees before I go," said the maiden of the green branch.

"But the sun is almost overhead," said one girl. "Won't your mother beat you if you do not come?"

"Beat? What is that? No one ever beats me," she replied indifferently. "You carry the linen home for me, and I will come when I have had my little nap. Good-by, my friends," and she waved them a farewell as she sat on the bank with her head on her hand, half reclining on the soft green grass in the shadow of the trees.

"Well, if that isn't Arletta!" said one young girl. "She commands us to carry home her linen for her, and we obey. We always do just what she tells us to. Listen! Now she is singing. If I stayed after the washing was done to sleep on the bank and to sing songs, I should have a sound beating, but Arletta always does what she likes." The maidens went slowly down the valley. Arletta half closed her eyes, and sang softly to herself.

"And may I listen to the pretty song?" said a voice coming so suddenly that it seemed to be just at her ear. Arletta sprang to her feet and made a humble courtesy, and then stood still, too abashed to look up. The rider had dismounted and stood holding his hat with its long plume in one hand and the horse's bridle in the other.

"Are you one of the maidens of Falaise?" he asked, and then smiled at the idle question, for where else could she belong?

"I'm Arletta," she answered, looking up shyly, "and my father is Fulbert the tanner."

"Strange that such a flower should blossom in the foul garden of a tanner," said Robert to himself.

"Are you the great Duke Richard?" asked the maiden.

"No, I'm not," said Robert half gloomily. "I'm nobody but Count Robert, his younger brother; and I haven't even a strong castle to bless myself with. But you must be tired. Isn't this washing too hard work for a girl like you?"

"Oh, no, I am strong," she said. "All the girls come out here to wash the linen for their homes."

"Shouldn't you rather stay at home and have some one to wash the linen for you? When you braid your hair, you could braid in a cord of shining gold, and you could wear a silken mantle and fasten it with a golden clasp."

"But it is only the great ladies in castles who wear silken mantles and braid gold in their hair," said Arletta, smiling, nevertheless, at the thought of so much luxury.

"And should you like to have a young man ride up on a great black horse to see you? He would have a feather in his hat, and perhaps he would wear a gold chain, if he is only a count, and he might bring you one day a jewelled band for your hair, and another day a veil of silken tissue, or perhaps a mantle of silk or of velvet. Should you like it?" Arletta said nothing, but her cheeks were bright red. Her eyes were bent on the ground, but when she ventured to look up for a moment, they were glittering with excitement.

"Farewell, my pretty Arletta," said he, "but it will not be many days before you will hear from me." He sprang upon his horse, kissed his hand to her gayly, and rode away, the horse's hoofs clattering on the fragments of stone in the road.

Whatever were Robert's faults, no one could accuse him of putting off what he meant to do, and it was only the next day when Fulbert came meekly from his tan-yard at the demand of the young noble.

"I have seen many a high-born maiden," said Robert without a word of explanation or preface, "and your daughter pleases me better than all of them. I would have her as the lady of the castle. Will you send her to me to-morrow?"

"The child of a tanner cannot well consort with the lord of a castle," said the father bravely, but with a trembling voice.

"And I have no castle worthy of the name," said Count Robert bitterly, "but I suppose that I may have a bride."

"The great folk have the power to take whom they will," said the tanner, his voice choking in his throat, "but I would have had my daughter wed one of her own station, and not in the castle but in the little church; and I wanted my kinsfolk and her mother's to look at her and smile upon her, and then to come to our house and rejoice that Arletta was going to her own home with the one that she had chosen."

"As you will," said the count, with pretended indifference; "but before you refuse, ask the girl herself. If she says no, I will leave her; but should she choose to say yes, you shall lose nothing by having your daughter the bride of a noble."

In the tiny inner room of the cottage stood Arletta, trembling and flushing.

"Hasten, Arletta," said her mother, Doda. "Hasten, and put on your best robe, the gray with the blue belt. He will go. A count will not wait long for a tanner's daughter. Tell him that you are ready—but, no; tell him that you will agree if—no, that will not do; ask him humbly if he would not rather that his bride were the daughter of a brewer than of a tanner; and tell him that if he would only give your father the gold to become a brewer, he would not be shamed that you have come from the home of a tanner."

"But perhaps I do not wish to go to the castle," said Arletta indifferently. "Perhaps I would rather walk to the church with all the village maidens, and have a wedding feast."

"Arletta, why will you torment me? Hasten; I do not hear a sound. Perhaps he is already gone. One would think you had no idea how great an honor it is. Don't you know that he can wed whom he will?"

"The one that weds me will be the one that *I* will," said Arletta.

"You are a proud, undutiful girl," said Doda. "Pull those folds more on the shoulders, and draw the girdle to the right. There, I hear his voice again. He has not gone."

"No, he has not gone," said Arletta, with a peculiar little smile, and she went forward slowly, till she stood in the opening between the two rooms. The soft gray garment hung in long folds from her shoulders, and was confined at the waist by a blue belt. Her cheeks were red, and her eyes shone.

"Go to him. Tell him you are sorry you have kept him so long," whispered Doda, twitching her daughter's robe, for she had crept up softly behind the girl. But Arletta did not take even a single step through the opening. She stood with one foot drawn back, as if she might disappear in a moment. So beautiful she was that Robert bent on one knee before her, and kissed her hand as if she had been some maiden of high degree.

"The next time that I see you, shall it be in the castle? Will you come to me, Arletta?"

"Say yes," whispered her mother, and even Fulbert had begun to realize that this was a great opportunity, and to fear lest the wayward damsel should refuse so lordly a suitor.

"Will you come, Arletta?" asked the count gently, looking eagerly into her eyes.

"Yes, I will come," said Arletta, with slow graciousness, and with a touch of condescension in manner that would have seemed to belong to a princess rather than to a simple maiden of the people. The count slipped about her neck a slender gold chain with a pearl in every link.

"That is to hold you fast," he said. "The castle is a grim and dreary place; but I know where there is a little door that leads to a chamber the thickness of the wall. It is dark and gloomy now, but people who are wise in using colors shall paint the walls with blue and gold and vermilion. The hangings shall be of silk, and every day the straw on the floor shall be bright with fresh flowers; and there shall you abide, and, tanner's daughter as you are, you shall be treated as if you were a king's daughter."

"Tell him you are grateful," whispered Doda anxiously, but Arletta only smiled slightly, with the air of one conferring a favor. The count sprang upon his great black horse, and went his way to the castle.

As he dropped his bridle into the hands of a servant, he asked:—

"And where is Ermenoldus?"

"Truly, my lord, I do not know," said the man. "He was here, and then he was not here, and when he was here he said, 'Tell my lord there is a message from me,' and then he was not here."

"Folly! no man could leave the castle unless the gate was opened for him. If you are telling me false, I'll have you thrown from the top of the cliff."

"Indeed, my lord, it is true," said the servant earnestly. "He was here, and then he was not here, and he said there was a message for you that you could read only in the glow of the fire."

"I believe the man is in league with the fiend," said Robert to himself. "To leave me just when I wanted him most!"

That night, when the count went to his bed, there lay on his pillow a scroll, closely tied with a golden cord that was wrought into an intricacy of many twists and coils. Impatiently he struggled with the knot.

"There's surely magic about it," he said, "and I have heard that if one cuts a magic knot, the wizardry will all turn against him," so he pulled and turned and twisted the golden thread, until all of a sudden it seemed to fly apart of its own accord under his fingers. Apparently nothing was written on the scroll, but as he held it half fearfully before the fire in the castle hall, there came out, letter by letter, a message. He read it slowly, for he was more used to reading the faces of men than lettering on parchment. It was this:—

"When one holds that which he would have, let him see to it that he hold it fast."

"Indeed I will," he said under his breath. "Arletta is mine, and the workmen shall work as never before, and if the little room in the tower is not ready in two days, some one shall go into the dungeon."

No one was thrown into the dungeon, for on the second day the little chamber in the wall was as bright and cheery as a place could be that had but a single window, and that a tiny one. However, people thought more of safety than of sunlight in those days, and the smallness of the opening was looked upon as an advantage. The frowning vaulting of the gray stonework that made the top of the room was hidden by a light blue coloring, half veiled by a graceful scrollwork of gold. All about the little window the stone was stained a deep, rich vermilion, and the walls were hung with heavy silken tapestries of a clear, sunny yellow. The floor was strewn with the softest of straw, and over it were sprinkled fresh roses from which the pages had removed every thorn. With precious stones—cut from the count's mantle of state—hung here and there on the walls, the little room flashed when the door was thrown open as if it was full of humming-birds.

All was ready, and Robert sent a chamberlain for Arletta. Behold, he returned without the village maiden!

"She would not come with me," he explained. "She said she would not come to the castle as a serving maid, she would come as the bride of a great lord; and she bade me return, if you were of the same mind, with an escort of palfreys well caparisoned, and with a due attendance. 'I do not go to the castle to beg,' she said—and O my lord, she looked like a queen when

11

she said it—'I go of my own will, and as the free maiden daughter of a gallant man. I will not creep up hill with a single chamberlain as my escort. If I am worth having, I am worth sending for in proper state. Then, too, the count has sent me no finely woven robe and no silken mantle. I have nothing save what is the gift of my father. Would he have me come to him wearing the gift of a tanner, or would he have me wear nothing at all but the little chain of gold and pearls?' Then she turned away, and I saw her no more." The count laughed.

"I like her the better for it," said he. "And now do you make up an escort as you would for the daughter of a duke. Carry her the handsomest tunic and mantle to be found in the castle. Choose the best palfreys, and have them as well groomed and as handsomely caparisoned as for a queen. Let twenty men-at-arms go with you, and see to it that you delay not in going. As for the coming, the fair Arletta will choose her own pace."

The little procession went forth and made its way along the rocky road to the home of the tanner. Robert watched it eagerly as it came slowly up the hill. At the castle gate there was a halt.

"Throw the gates open wide," he heard a low, clear voice say. "I am not an uninvited guest. I come here at the wish of the count and of my own free will."

"Let him see to it that he hold it fast," said Robert, "and that I will," and he hastened to welcome the fair Arletta.

Month after month passed away, but the charm of the tanner's daughter for the young count did not grow less. Whether she met him in her plain gray gown, with the playful humility of a village maiden, or in the rich robes of the lady of the castle, to whom all must do honor, and with a pride and haughtiness equal to that of the count's aristocratic grandfather, Richard the Fearless, she was equally fascinating to Count Robert. His brother's interests were forgotten. Of his own he took no heed. It began to be whispered that he would not willingly depart from the castle of Falaise.

Now Normandy and the districts round about were swarming with people, too many for even so fertile a country to nourish. The land had been divided and subdivided until the share of a man would no longer support those who were in helpless dependence upon him. There was restlessness everywhere. The women of the household must abide at home; nowhere else was there protection or safety. The fathers of families must struggle on as best they could; but the young men were held back by no question of fear, bound by no demands of any who were dependent upon them. From one domain to another they wandered, ready to throw themselves vehemently into whatever cause might come to hand. They were any man's soldiers if he would pay them well. They would follow the sound of the tinkling silver wherever it might lead.

The country about was full of such men, and at the first whisper of the count's unwillingness to leave Falaise, they hastened to the castle. The weapon lay at

Robert's hand. Would he use it? One of the boldest of the young soldiers made his way to the count.

"Here we are," he said, "and here are our weapons. Can you make use of us and of them? We will fight for you bravely and faithfully."

CHAPTER II

THE BANQUET AT ROUEN

G IVE a child a knife and its first thought is to cut. So it was with the count. Here he was in a castle that ought to be his. Its walls were solid, its keep was massy. Men who were eager to fight under his banner were pressing upon him. What should hinder him from holding fast to his own?

"I wish Ermenoldus was here," he thought. Then his mind wandered back to the last time that he had seen the wizard, as he called him, and more than half in earnest.

"We were talking about the castle and its thick walls and the great precipice below it," he thought, "and then he disappeared and left me the mysterious message that I could read only in the glow of the fire." Ever since the strange guest had departed, Robert had carried the little scroll in his bosom. He drew it out and read it anew. Another interpretation flashed upon him.

"The castle of Falaise is that which I 'would have,'" he said aloud. "'Let him see to it that he hold it fast.' That will I do. Brother or demon, duke or king, let them come on. Here is my castle—*my* castle—and here are bold fighters, and up there in the little room in the thickness of the wall is as beautiful a lady to fight for as ever sat on a royal throne. Here I am and here will I remain." In an hour the castle was in commotion. There was a great polishing of shields and spears. Armor that had grown rusty in the time of quiet, so unusual in those stormy days, was rubbed and strengthened and its breaks repaired. The forges blazed night and day. War-horses were to be shod. Arrowheads were to be made. Swords were to be sharpened to a keen edge that would cut through head and helmet at a blow. Axes were ground, and the helve of each was carefully tested, for on its strength might depend a fighter's chance of life or the defence of the castle gate.

In the midst of all the eager preparations, a man appeared at the gate. He was muddy. His shoes were in fragments, and his clothes were torn to rags by the thick briers through which he had forced his way; but when he spoke, men listened as if their lives hung upon his words. The words were few, they were only these:—

"Duke Richard and a great force are coming through the forest at the other side of the town."

Robert's first thought was of the security of the fair bride whom he had taken from the home of her father. In general, the keep of a castle was the safest place in a siege, but in this instance, when a duke was trying to regain possession of his own, then, however much he might be forced to injure the castle, he would do no needless damage to the peasants living on his land. The best place for Arletta was in her father's house, and there she was carried with as much of form and ceremony as the hasty departure would permit.

Hardly had the castle gate been closed upon the return of the men who had acted as her escort, when the glitter of the spears of Richard's soldiers was seen in the distance. Nearer and nearer they came. First rode the standard-bearer and the guards of the standard. Then came the duke himself, with flashing helmet and shield and coat of mail, his armorial bearings blazoned on even the trappings of his horse. The coat of mail was in one piece, and was shaped like a tunic, falling to the knees, and protecting his arms down to the wrists. His legs were guarded by wide thongs of leather crossed and recrossed. To the broad belt that fell across his shoulder hung a dirk and a short, stout sword. His shield was oblong, rounded at the top and narrowing to a point at the bottom. That there should be no little crevice where an unfriendly lance might enter, his coat of mail had a kind of hood, also of mail, that covered the back of his head to the helmet, and shielded his cheeks. He carried a lance, and from its head waved the gonfalon, or pennant, around which his men were to rally at the call of their lord.

The knights who accompanied Richard were armed and equipped in much the same way, save that their accoutrements were less rich, and not always as complete. Around each knight were grouped his own vassals, whom he was required to arm and mount and lead in the service of the duke.

No coat of mail had the men of low degree. That belonged to the knights, and every one knew that a man of humble birth could never be worthy of being made a knight. They were allowed to wear a stuffed tunic that afforded some little protection, and under it they might have a sort of breastplate of leather. They carried a round shield. Their weapons were the lance, the battle-axe, the bow, the sling, even clubs and flails and maces, and staves with prongs. They were permitted to carry a sword, but it must be long and slender— not short and thick like that of the nobles. Together with these vassals were many of the same eager, restless adventurers that had entered the service of Robert.

Up the winding road came the troops of Richard, closer and closer to the castle. Robert's men stood on the wall hurling down great stones, firing deadly arrows, and thrusting back with their long lances the foremost men in the ranks of the duke. The contest was the more bitter in that the foes were brothers. Wild shouts arose from both sides—of rage from one and defiance from the other. Richard's arbalests, unwieldy machines for hurling great stones, drove Robert's men down from the walls; or rather their dead bodies were dragged down by their fellow-fighters to make room for other men. The outer walls were captured, and there was a pause.

Robert's men were few, and there was no way to make good his losses; while Richard's followers had been more in number at first, and additions had been continually coming up. The walls of the donjon were thick and heavy, but the art of using stone as a material for castle-building was in its infancy, and there were weaknesses in the structure of which a determined assailant might take advantage. After the moment's rest, Richard's men were rousing themselves for a final attack, and this, Robert knew, could hardly fail to be successful. He stood with grim, set face, and around him gathered his fighters, watching him, and ready to obey the least indication of his wishes.

"It is of no use. The castle must yield," said Robert gloomily.

"True, my lord," said a grave voice behind him.

"Ermenoldus! wizard that you are, give me your aid. How came you here?"

"I wish I was a wizard, my lord," said Ermenoldus sadly. "I would run the risk of the flame and the fagot if I could help you, for I have done you nothing but harm when I meant to work you good."

"But how came you here?"

"By no wizardry, my lord. There is a tiny crevice under a jutting rock which is hidden by bushes. A slender man like me can easily make his way up the crack, for it is scarcely more than that. A sudden twist, a writhing through a little gap between the foundation rocks, and I am in your fortress. It was as well that your servants should think it witchcraft. Unrevealed knowledge is unshared power."

"'Is there no hope, Ermenoldus?"

"None, my lord. To save yourself from death— no, perhaps not death, that is easy—but from a life in the lowest depths of the castle dungeon, you must yield. Take down your standard. Put up the white flag and sue for peace. Make what terms you can, but yield."

The white flag was put up, and in the gloomy keep of the castle, red and slippery with the blood of slaughtered men, the two brothers debated again the question of the heritage—Richard calmly, as with the manner of a man who did but claim his own; Robert gloomily, but with a certain ready meekness that might have made those who knew him best question whether all his thoughts were made clear by his words. The end of the discussion was this: Robert might have the district of the Hiesmois, and hold it free from his brother's interference, but the castle of Falaise must still belong to Richard.

All was quiet and concord. The soldiers marched to Richard's capital, Rouen, the two brothers riding together at the head of their men. A great banquet was made ready in the castle—a strange mixture of luxury and discomfort. The chairs of that day were heavy and clumsy. At family dinners people sat on stools, but at a ceremonious feast like this benches were used, and the guests huddled together as best they could. There were nutcrackers, but there were no forks. Warriors noted for their bravery were given bulls' horns bound with rings of silver or of gold for their drinking cups, and these were filled over and over again with beer or wine. There were vegetables of many kinds, fish of all varieties, rabbits, fowl, venison, and lamb. Pork appeared in the shape of ham, sausages, black pudding, and roast. It was the most common meat, though it was often eaten with a little fear lest it should produce leprosy.

For dessert there were baked fruits and nuts of all the kinds that could be obtained, cheese, red and white sugar-plums, and on a raised platform in the middle of the table were jellies, elaborately fashioned in the shape of a swan, heron, bittern, or peacock. The real peacock was the dish of honor, and was called the "food for the brave." It was stuffed and roasted. Its beak was gilded with gold, and sometimes its whole body was covered with silver gilt. The bird was brought in with a waving of banners, and a flourish of trumpets like that which announced the coming of some great dignitary.

The feast was elaborate, but it was served with no attempt at any special order. After orange preserves came chickens, and after lamb sausages came a delicate pie made of larks. Nuts were quite likely to appear before ham, and sweet jellies before soup.

Such a banquet as this required a kitchen of generous dimensions, and so it was that the kitchen of a noble must have great spits on which many joints of different kinds could be roasted, together with whole sheep and venison and long rows of poultry. There must be many utensils, and in the houses of men of highest rank there was a special servant to take care of the copper dishes, kettles, saucepans, and caldrons, and to see to it that they were safe and bright and shining.

The banquet hall was lighted by hanging lamps, and lamps on standards, and countless wax candles set in chandeliers and in candlesticks. The walls were hung with finely woven tapestries. Within the hall there was a barbaric sort of luxury, but in the town in which the hall of feasting stood, the pigs were still running wild in the streets.

When men began to weary of feasting, jugglers and minstrels came in to amuse them. The minstrels sang to the music of a sort of double-barrelled flute, or recited long poems of war or adventure in doggerel rhymes. Lavish gifts were presented to them, and they went away rejoicing in generous sums of money, or clothing of scarlet or violet cloth, or in fur robes or jewels or noble horses.

The jugglers were treated equally well, and perhaps the amusements which they provided were even more generally appreciated by the guests. These jugglers performed all sorts of sleight-of-hand tricks. They boxed and they wrestled and they danced. They threw up lances and caught them by the point, or they spun naked swords over their heads and caught the flashing weapons as they fell. Then, too, they led about bears and monkeys and dogs that fought or danced together. The dogs would walk about on their hind legs, the monkeys would ride horseback, while the bears pretended to be dead and the goats played on the harp.

Hour after hour the feasting and the amusements and the rejoicing continued. Every one drank the health of every one else. Especially friendly and harmonious did the two brothers appear, who had so recently fought together as the deadliest of foes. In many a golden-bound horn of wine they pledged each other. At last the time came when men could feast no more. The words of farewell were said, and the banquet was over. Scarcely had the festival lights been extinguished when the bells began to toll for the sudden death of Richard. Robert returned to Falaise. The castle was his, and he was Duke of Normandy.

The new duke began his reign by a generosity that made his followers rejoice.

"He's the duke for me," said one of them jubilantly. "Duke Richard gave me one suit a year, and Duke Robert will give me two."

"Yes," said a second retainer, "when Arcy showed him his sword all dinted and bent in the fight and asked for another, he gave him a sword and a new coat of mail and a fine new horse and a helmet."

"Was that what killed Arcy? Did he die of joy?"

"That is what some one said, but I think he ate too much at the feast, and they didn't bleed him soon enough."

"Perhaps he drank of the wrong cup by mistake," said another, with a significant look.

"I don't quarrel with any duke that doubles my salary," said the first. "He is my friend who shows himself a friend, and I'll stand by Robert the Magnificent. Richard died, to be sure; but then he might have been killed in the battle so it would have been all the same now."

It mattered little to Robert who was pleased and who was displeased at his accession. He was duke, and he meant to rule, and that was enough. Falaise pleased him. The hunting was good, the castle was the strongest in his domain; it was the place for which he had fought, and now that it was in his hands, he meant to keep it. Moreover, in the home of a man who had once been a tanner, there was the fairest lady in the duchy. It seemed best that she should remain for a while in her father's house. Those were stormy times, and until Robert's position was perfectly established, she would be more safe from secret foes in the humbler home of her parents than in the castle itself, with all its mighty walls and its store of weapons.

He had lost one upon whom he had been more than a little inclined to rely—the "wizard" Ermenoldus—and in a way to make him feel the loss the more keenly. Ermenoldus had accused certain nobles of being unfaithful to Robert. One by one they challenged him to single combat. One by one they were defeated, but at last in a final duel with a forester he was slain. Sorrow, pleasure, anxiety, triumph, contended in Robert's mind. It is no wonder that he was restless and uneasy.

"One would think that the great folks might let us sleep of nights," said a peasant woman sleepily to her husband, as she turned wearily on the heap of straw that was their bed.

"That was the duke," said her husband. "Listen! you can hear his horse's hoof-beats even now, and he must be almost up to the castle. He gallops faster than any one else."

"Why can't he do his galloping by day?" grumbled the woman. "They take our cattle, and they make us work in their fields and on their roads. If we turn around we have to pay a tax, and if we stand still, we have to pay a tax. They might let us sleep at night."

"Perhaps the duke cannot sleep either," said the peasant; and he added significantly: "It is not good to fight with one's brother. I have heard that if a man does, little demons will come at night and torment him."

"Perhaps evil spirits made him do it," said the wife making the sign of the cross; but the husband said:—

"I don't believe he is a very good man, for they say that sometimes he burns a whole armful of wax candles in a night, because he won't be in the dark."

"Well, everybody knows that wax candles ought to be given to the church," said the wife.

"A wizard used to come to see him sometimes," said the man, "and no one knew how he ever got into the castle or how he got out of it. The porter said that once when the wizard was standing close to him and the gate was shut, he looked away for just a minute, and when he turned, the wizard was gone; but when he opened the gate half an hour later, the wizard was going down the hill as free as might be, and the porter declared that when the man waved his hand, he could see a streak of fire."

"It might have been his ghost," said the woman.

"It might *now*," said her husband, "but he wasn't dead then. Mayhap, though, it was his ghost that fought the— No, he was not dead then, either. They used to say that he could make a vine grow fast or slow as he would, and that if he looked at you over the right shoulder, you would have good luck, but that if he looked at you over the left shoulder, whatever you planted would die or your house would burn down or the spring would dry up or something bad would come to you. I have heard that if he said some good words over the ground, there would be a great harvest, and that if he shook his head at the moon and said something that no one could understand, any one that went out into the moonlight that night would fall down dead."

"Duke Richard fell down dead right after the great feast, didn't he? They say that the wizard was there."

"No, he wasn't there; but what happened then is why they call the duke 'Robert the Devil.' They say it was only Richard and the very bravest of his knights that died, and that not one of Duke Robert's men was hurt."

"I think it was all that wizard," said the wife positively. "A wizard can do things if he isn't there; and then he might have been there, even if they couldn't see him. A wizard doesn't have to be seen if he doesn't choose to be. He might have looked at the wine over the left shoulder. Duke Robert is kind and good, I am sure of that, for when he was riding at full speed one day, Pierre's little girl stood still in the road right in front of his horse. He had a right to run over her, of course, but he dashed out among those great stones just at the turn of the road and did not harm her at all. And there's something more to tell, for instead of going down on her knees and thanking him for sparing her life, the silly little thing only opened her mouth and cried at the top of her voice."

"Didn't he even tell some one to beat her?"

"No, that he did not; he bent away down from the saddle—and he might have fallen off and rolled down the bank and been killed; only think of it, the duke killed for the child of a serf!—he bent down from the saddle and caught her up. The mother thought he was going to throw her down over the rocks, and she began to cry too; but he gave the child a ride on that great black horse of his, and then lifted her down and filled both her hands with red and white sugar-plums, the kind that they say great folks have at their feasts. No one in the village ever saw any before, and all the people around here have been in to see them. The child is so proud that when she plays with the other children, she is all the time saying, 'You never rode on the great black horse'; and really her mother isn't much better, for she says her daughter shall never marry any man who isn't at least a free-man."

"She will marry the one that the duke chooses, of course," said the husband; "but she was certainly a fortunate child. Not many nobles would have let her off so easily when she was right in the road. Perhaps it was the wizard, after all, and Duke Robert had nothing to do with the wine."

"I heard one of the knights call the duke 'Robert the Magnificent,' " said the woman.

"And I heard one call him 'Robert the Devil,' " said the man.

"I suppose the great folks have some way of knowing which is right," said the woman, and then they went to sleep.

More than once that night did the great black horse gallop up and down the winding road between the castle and the village below the hill. More than once did the rider in his restlessness fling himself from the saddle and stride impatiently up and down in front of his stronghold. Then he would mount again and ride furiously down the hill, the hoofs of his horse striking fire on the stones in his path.

CHAPTER III

FROM CASTLE TO COTTAGE

I N the village, not far from the market-place, was the home of Fulbert, made larger and more comfortable. To keep out the cold draughts, the walls were hung with tapestry, a refinement of luxury never seen before in the cottage of a peasant, so that the little house was the wonder of all the people in the vicinity. There was also a chair, a real chair; clumsy and heavy, to be sure, but there was gilt on it, and the arms were carved, and, moreover, it was the only chair in the neighborhood, and that was fame. The family sat on stools at the table, of course; but then every one knew that they could use a chair if they chose.

Doda was not at all averse to letting her friends have a glimpse of her cooking utensils, and report said that some of them were made of copper, "Just as if they were in a king's kitchen," said the admiring people. When Fulbert and his family ate their dinner, they did not use plain wooden trenchers as did their neighbors, but a kind of pottery with thick, heavy glazing. They drank from wooden cups, to be sure, but the cups were edged with a rim of silver; and most astounding luxury of all, rumor said that they actually had all the wax candles that they chose to burn.

More than one armful of them was burned on the night that Duke Robert rode so furiously up and down the long hill. By and by all was still in the cottage. The duke was quiet in the castle, but before the sun was far above the horizon, he was again at the foot of the hill, and softly entering the door of the little house.

"Here he is, my lord, here he is," said the old nurse, "and he's even a lustier boy by daylight than he was by candlelight. It's a good thing that light of a wax candle shone on him first, for bees gather wax, and so he will be rich and powerful. Here's your boy, my lord," and she put the baby into the arms of its father, and drew aside the curtain that separated the outer from the inner room where Arletta lay. The duke would have known what to do on a battlefield with an enemy before him and with a sword in his hand, but with his quick-witted, sparkling Arletta lying pale and weak, and in his arms the little red bundle that seemed heavier than a suit of armor, he was as helpless as any other young father who is not a duke. Arletta smiled gently, and whispered:—

"Is he not a fine boy?"

"Indeed he is," said the duke, "and I'll do more for him than any one thinks. But what makes him shut up his hands so tight? Is anything the matter?" he said to the nurse.

"All babies do," said the nurse composedly, "but all babies don't do what he did last night; for when we laid him on the straw, he clutched a handful and he held on to it, and when he was put on the bed to sleep, he kept it in his hand, he did; and that means something, it does. Everybody that's had to do with babies knows that."

"What does it mean?" asked Duke Robert, looking at the nurse as if she alone could speak the words of wisdom.

"This is what it means—and it isn't myself alone that says it, for I heard my mother's mother say it when I was no higher than *that*—that whatever thing a child does first, that will he always do; and this child will reach out and take to himself, and what he takes he will hold, until the time comes that he will have more than any one dreams of."

"That is the tree in your dream," said Robert, turning to Arletta.

"Yes, and dreams mean something, too," said the nurse, who was so elated at having the duke for a listener that she had no idea when to stop. "When the lady Arletta told me what a dream she had had, that a tree arose from her body, and its branches spread out till they shaded all Normandy, *I* knew what it meant; and *I* knew what it meant when the boy clutched the straw. He's no common child."

"No, he's not," said the duke, looking at the baby with much respect mingled with a little alarm, for it was puckering up its face to do the duke knew not what; and when the first cry came forth, the warlike

noble who never fled from his foes actually dropped
his son into the nurse's arms and made his way into
the open air as rapidly as possible, feeling very big and
clumsy, and really trembling and glancing around him
in dismay when his sword knocked against the heavy
oaken chair in his hurried escape.

One week after its birth the baby was taken to
the parish church to be baptized. Never before had
there been such an assemblage to see the baptism of
any infant. Falaise was quite an important place, not
only because of its castle, but on account of its trade in
leather and its manufacture of woollens. The people
were not all humble peasants, some among them were
well-to-do; and the country round about, rich in flocks
and herds, was the home of many a prosperous vassal.
The herdsmen left their flocks and the weavers their
looms, the peasants willingly ran the risk of fines and
penalties, and all flocked to the church to see the baptism of the child of a great noble. What would be his
name? The crowds that pressed around the font had
been all eyes, but when the priest asked:—

"What is the name of this child?" then they
were all ears. They need not have been afraid of losing
a word, for in a great voice that rang throughout the
church Duke Robert said:—

"His name shall be William, and let all men
know that he is named for William of the Long Sword,
his ancestor."

Just within the church door was another William, one William Talvas, Earl of Belesme, who stood
with angry eyes and grim, stern face.

THE BAPTISM OF WILLIAM THE CONQUEROR

"You have a namesake, Earl William," said the burgess of a neighboring town, who stood near him. "How do you like the robust son of your liege lord?"

"Shame on him, shame on him!" said the haughty chieftain bitterly. "My grandfather was a faithful friend of Robert's grandfather, and did him good service; and now for the sake of the whining grandson of a tanner, I and mine will be put to loss and dishonor. May shame and disgrace be his lot as long as he shall live!" and William Talvas, without waiting for the rest of the ceremony, flung himself out of the church and galloped furiously away, as if the very air of Falaise was poisoned by the little child at the font.

Arletta was soon taken to the stone castle, together with her father, mother, and her brother Walter, for Robert, in his delight at having in arms the "fair young son" for whom he had longed could not do enough for the lady and her family.

It was a gloomy place. Thick walls surrounded it, pierced by a formidable gate. Over the gateway was the heavy iron portcullis, ready to be dropped in a moment at the approach of a foe or a stranger; for in those times of sudden alarms any unknown man was a foe until he had shown himself a friend. Within the walls was a courtyard that might have been bright and pleasant, had it not been for the grim stone bulwarks that seemed to shut it away from all the cheerful, sunny world without. Here stood the keep. In its lowest depths were the cellars and the dungeons, where a lord might fling his captive enemies; and there, unless their friends were stronger than he, he might keep them without word or interference, until their bones strewed the damp stone floors that had been wet with the blood of many a wounded prisoner before them.

Above the dungeons was the hall. The windows were mere slits in the walls, so that the sunlight rarely entered; but there was a great cheery blaze in the fireplace, and it was the very heart of home to the feudal lord. Here the family sat. Here the lady of the castle and her maidens embroidered the lord's coat of arms on his standard, or, with the bright colors gleaming in the light of many candles, worked on the rich tapestries that were to be the comfort and the beauty of the home. Here the children of the family played about the glowing fire; and here the girls were taught to care for the sick and the wounded, to make the decorations for robes of ceremony, and to do all that might fall to the share of the lady of a castle. The boys made bows and arrows and wooden spears, and held mimic tournaments in the further corners of the great room. Then they would all gather around the father of the family as he told of some success in the hunting field; and the dogs, lying as near the fire as they had been able to press their way, would prick up their ears as they heard their names, and understood that it was their deeds that their master was praising.

Even more attentively did the household listen to the lord when he told of some warlike exploit, the repulse of an assault, or a successful attack upon some distant castle. Then the children would gather closer, and the lady would drop her embroidery, for when her lord was away, she was defender of the castle; her commands were obeyed, and it would be her skill or her ignorance that would save her home or lose it.

Duke Robert had made Fulbert his chamberlain, or guardian of the ducal robes of state, while the son Walter seems to have been a special watchman to care for the safety of his little nephew; for even when the child was in the cradle, there was more than one fierce warrior who, noting the duke's fondness for his son, feared loss to him and his, and would gladly have seen injury or death come to the grandchild of the tanner.

In this little time of peace Robert was happier than at any other period of his stormy life; but his happiness was soon interrupted, and by his own relatives. Robert was a hard rider, a ready fighter, and utterly fearless in time of danger. There were many possibilities that such a man would die by an early and violent death. Several of these relatives had counted upon their chances of succeeding to the inheritance; but with his devotion to the child at his castle, their hopes grew less, and they were the more ready to find cause of resentment in real or fancied wrongs. Some one whispered to Robert that his uncle, the Archbishop of Rouen, was assembling large numbers of fighting men at his own town of Evreux. Without waiting many days to inquire into the rights of the case, and whether or not there was actual danger of a revolt, Robert marched straightway against his warlike uncle, and besieged his stronghold so vigorously that the fighting prelate thought it best to take refuge under the sheltering care of the king of France.

As a warrior he had failed to overpower his energetic nephew, so he took what seems a rather unfair advantage of his priestly authority, and excommunicated him as a rebel against the church. By this decree all persons were forbidden to offer him food or shelter. They were to avoid him, as one whose touch would infect them with some deadly disease; and if mortal illness came upon him, he was to be buried without word of prayer or religious ceremony. Nor was this all, for the archbishop also laid Robert's duchy under an interdict. The churches were to be closed, no bells could be rung—and no one knew how many evil spirits might be hovering in the air that the sound of a church-bell would have dispersed—no marriage could receive the blessing of the church and no burial rites could be performed.

Even if this decree was not carried out with the most literal obedience, any duke, be he as fearless as the great Rollo himself, might well wish to make terms with an enemy who used such thunderbolts as his weapons. Peace was made between them, the archbishop was invited to return to Rouen—and Robert straightway fell into similar difficulties with another priestly relative, Hugh, Bishop of Bayeux. He, too, shut himself up in a stronghold, but Robert besieged him so effectually that he yielded.

More trouble was yet to come. Following the custom of the land, Robert, on his accession, had sent for his vassals to do him homage and swear to be faithful to him. Among them was William Talvas of Belesme. The old earl was not the man to change his mind lightly, and his scorn of Robert's child was as bitter as ever. With sullen rage the earl and his four sons debated what should be done.

"Never will I do homage to the father of the brat that I saw in the church!" said the earl. "There's no priest and there's no church that can free the grandson of a vile tanner from stain," he thundered; "and I'll swear no fealty and I'll do no homage to the man whose chamberlain is a tanner, the man who sits in his own hall beside a tanner's son, the man who is father to a tanner's grandchild. A tanner! A skinner of dead beasts! The meanest, lowest, most contemptible of all trades! There is not a serf in Alençon that does not despise it. Call out our fighters! Fill the castle with arms! Strengthen the walls and the gates, and make the dungeons deeper!" and the old man sank upon a bench, exhausted by his own rage.

His orders were obeyed. The earl and his four sons and many other brave fighters shut themselves up in the stronghold of Alençon. Robert's forces drew nearer. They surrounded the walls. They pressed closer and closer, so indomitable that the earl had no hope of victory, so watchful that he had no chance of escape. Fulk was slain, Robert, the second son, was severely wounded; and still, drawn up closely around the fortress, stood that line of resolute fighters. The earl yielded, and asked permission to beg pardon and to take the oath of fealty.

Now it had become a custom in the land that an unfaithful vassal should be forgiven only after great humiliations. The earl, never yielding in thought, whatever his lips might say, must stand before his conqueror, barefooted, half naked, with a horse's saddle strapped to his shoulders, and beg pardon for his unfaithfulness. This the earl did, trembling with cold as well as with rage.

The Duke of Normandy had become a man of power. His duchy had a matchless sea-coast. It bordered upon several of the great lordships that were some day to form a united France. It manufactured arms and cutlery and woollen goods, and it was rich in agricultural products. Its revenues flowed in so generously that even a lavishness like Robert's failed to affect them. The rightful king of the district then known as France looked upon the duke as his most potent friend. Great need had he of friends, for his mother, his younger brother, and a strong party were against him. The helpless king, fleeing from his enemies with an escort of only twelve attendants, came to Robert, his vassal, and begged for help to gain possession of his own kingdom.

Robert received the suppliant king with such honors and such richness of entertainment that he well merited the name of "Robert the Magnificent"; but no less did he deserve the title of "Robert the Devil" from his savage punishment of those who had rebelled against their sovereign. Henry's gratitude was equal to Robert's services, and he gave his ally a strip of borderland called the Vexin. Robert's dominions now extended almost to the city of Paris; and henceforth Normandy and France must stand or fall together.

In these stormy times the home of Arletta and her children, for now there was also a little daughter, had been by turns the frowning castle of grim gray stone at the brink of the precipice, and the sunny little cottage in the valley below it. When the duke was at home, they were with him in the castle; but when he was absent on his war-like expeditions, it was safer for them to be where in case of need they could more readily find a hiding-place among the homes of the poor. There was also another reason. When the lord was away, the lady of the castle must take command, as has been said before, if her home was attacked by enemies. When Robert was by the side of Arletta, he could bear down upon all disobedience with a heavy hand, and punish with the utmost severity the least disrespect shown to the mother of his child; but he knew well that in his absence not one of all his men-at-arms would obey the orders of a tanner's daughter. There would be rebellion and insurrection. It might be that the duke would lose his favorite castle.

So it was that the earliest memories of the little William were of being carried hurriedly from castle to cottage or from cottage to castle. He would hear the din of armor and the clashing of swords and spears. Then the duke, with a great company following him, would ride away on his war-horse, and when the little boy asked:—

"But, my mother, where is my father?" the answer would be:—

"He is fighting for the king of France," or "He has gone away to kill the men that wanted to kill him."

"And will he come home to Adelaide and me when he has killed them?"

"Yes," his mother would say.

"Then I hope he will kill a great many, and kill them very soon, so that he will come back to see us," the little boy would answer wistfully.

When the duke was on the return, his little son would listen for the first hoof-beats of his horse, and even if it was in the night, he would awake and call out joyfully:—

"Did you kill many men, father? Will anybody try to kill you if you stay with us now?" Then they would go to the castle, and there would be a feast in the great hall. The firelight would sparkle and glow, and flash upon the rows of shields and the clusters of spears on the wall. The child thought that the weird pictures which it made were the faces of the people that had been killed, and that they were trying to come down to sit at the long table and share the feast.

"You won't let them come down, will you, father?" he asked, pointing to the shields above his head.

"No," said his father, "but you shall have a shield if you like, and a sword, too." So the little boy had a tiny suit of armor made of quilted linen with metal rings sewn thickly over it, and a helmet and a lance and a sword and a little shield. When they were all on, they were so heavy that he could hardly stand, but he would stagger about happily under their weight and say proudly:—

"Now I'm a soldier just like my father, and when I'm a man, I'm going to ride on a big horse, and go off to kill people just as he does."

The nobles might refuse, so far as they dared, to allow their sons to be playmates of the grandson of a tanner; but to the children of the well-to-do burghers of Falaise it was an honor to play with the son of a duke; and the boys readily allowed the little fellow to take the lead in their games, and when he said:—

"I don't want to play marbles," or "I don't want to spin tops," they were ready to do whatever he suggested. One day he said:—

"I don't want to play morra, I don't want to hold my fingers up any more. I want to do what my father does and have some soldiers."

"But *we* haven't any swords," said the boys, who had often envied the son of the duke his military outfit.

"My father will give you some if I ask him," he said confidently. And so it was, for soon every boy was provided with some kind of weapons or armor, and the little child became commander of a company of children. Up and down they marched to orders which the little fellow thought were like those that his father gave. One day he suddenly stood still and said:—

"My father doesn't go up and down the road. He takes castles. He said he did. We'll go and take the castle." So straight up to the gate marched the line of boys, led by their proud little commander. He beat upon the wall with the hilt of his tiny sword, and the porter began to swing open the gate.

"No, that isn't the way," said the boy indignantly. "Shut the gate and go and tell the duke to come down." The man obeyed, and the duke came at the command of this new sovereign. The little boy marched up to him with as long strides as his heavy armor and his short legs would permit and called out:—

"Are you the duke?"

"Yes," said his father in amazement.

"We've come to take the castle, and we'll kill everybody if you don't surrender."

The duke surrendered.

CHAPTER IV

ROBERT THE PILGRIM

"I am the grandson of Richard the Fearless as well as he, and I will never do homage to my proud cousin." So said Alain of Brittany, and again the little boy saw his father mount the great war-horse, and ride swiftly down the hill. He was followed by a troop of fighters, for there were plenty of men who would do anything for money, and Robert had "sous of Rouen" enough to hire as large an army as he chose.

When his little son saw the preparations, he straightway asserted his right to go with the company.

"I am a soldier, too," he said, "and you let the other soldiers go. I have a sword and a coat of mail, and I can give the commands—you know I can. I've taken a castle, too. You know you had to surrender. Won't you let me go?"

"A soldier must ride a horse," said the duke, "and you can only ride a pony. The next time I go out to fight, then, if you are big enough to ride a horse, perhaps I will take you with me.—I believe the youngster would be as brave as "any old fighter," he muttered to himself proudly.

Alain, too, had summoned his vassals—men of high rank, brave warriors with a brave leader—and yet, when Robert's men dashed upon them, suddenly rushing up from the glen where they had been hidden, they fled for their lives. The enemy pursued, hunted them down like wolves, killed horse and rider without mercy, until more than half the noble army had been slain. There was one more expedition against Alain—an angry, pitiless campaign. Would Alain submit, or did he prefer, first to have his land devastated, and then to submit? Alain yielded, and did homage. Then he turned sullenly to leave the presence of the duke, but Robert called him back.

"Alain, my cousin," said he, "I have fought you as fiercely as I know how to fight, for I was holding to what I believe is my lawful due. Do you blame me for that?"

"Every man has a right to his own," said Alain evasively; but the duke had more to say.

"I thought it was mine. You thought it was yours. We fought it out fairly and squarely, and I have won. Do you bear malice for the result of an honest fight?"

"No," said Alain hesitatingly.

"I have made my own way," said the duke. "I have never sought aid or favor or advice from any man. This is the first time that I have asked a man for his friendship, but now I want a friend, not a conquered enemy. Will you give me your hand and swear to be, not my vassal, but my friend?" Alain turned slowly toward the duke. Then he glanced at his cousin's face. There was an appealing look that no one had ever seen before on the countenance of the proud noble. The fiery, warm-hearted Alain melted in an instant. He laid his hand in that of the duke, and said:—

"I will be your friend, and whatever you ask in the name of our friendship, that will I do."

"I thank you from the bottom of my heart," said Robert; "and the time may come when I shall ask the greatest favor that one man could ask of another in this the duchy of Normandy, and I shall trust you as never before did one man trust another." Then in a moment, Robert was the same proud, headstrong, self-sufficient man that he had always been, and for a while Alain almost fancied that those few minutes had been a dream.

It was but a short time after this that Robert called together the earls and barons and bishops and abbots of his duchy, every man of mark among those who paid him homage. In their robes of state they came to the appointed place, each one followed by a company of armed men. It was a brilliant assemblage. There was the Archbishop of Rouen, the uncle with whom Robert had fought, and whom he had afterward made chief of his council, and there was his cousin, Alain of Brittany.

No one could even guess why they had been summoned. They knew of no question great enough to call out the whole ducal council. Not one of them had the least suspicion of what was to come, nor would they have known any better even if they had heard the duke's last command to a chamberlain just before he entered the council room. It was this:—

"'When you hear me strike three times with the hilt of my sword, bring in my son; and see to it that he is dressed in the richest attire that the castle will furnish." Then the duke entered the room where the whole dazzling company awaited his presence. After the usual forms of opening a council of state had been completed, then, without word of introduction, Robert expressed his will.

"It is well to be duke of a wide realm," said he, "but one must care for the good of his soul. I have sinned, and I must do penance, or else suffer forever and ever the punishment due to my misdeeds."

"He is going to resign the kingdom," thought the councillors, and more than one of them formed in a moment a scheme to secure the dukedom for himself. But Robert went on:—

"There is one way by which a man may wipe away even the darkest crime, and that way will I take. This is what I will do. Bare-headed, bare-footed, in the guise of a pilgrim, and with staff in hand, I will go to Jerusalem; and when once my feet have trodden on the holy ground, then shall I be freed from my sins. Then will I return and rule my duchy—and woe to him who has been an unfaithful vassal. I shall find means to make him regret his falseness," said the duke haughtily, for humility was not exactly his most prominent virtue. Then arose one of his relatives.

"Duke Robert, my cousin," said he, "I am most heartily sorry that such a thought has entered your mind. I can only guess whom we have to thank for this," and he glanced toward the Archbishop of Rouen, "but I am safe in saying that if any one has had a hope of gain for himself in persuading—"

"My thoughts are my own," said the duke proudly. "If there is any one here who can say that he had word or whisper of my plan before this day, let him speak." There was silence for a moment, then another councillor arose.

"A lordless land is open to every foe," he said. "Normandy is strong, but we have on every side territories that are envious of her wealth, of her power, of her alliance with King Henry of France. We have brave leaders, and we can call out brave soldiers, but what is all our bravery without a commander who holds his place by a right that none can dispute? It is well to cleanse one's self from sin, but shall our land fall into revolt and ruin that it may be done so hastily? Duke Robert, you are a young man, let the pilgrimage wait. In years to come, if you would make a pilgrimage, you can leave us in quiet fealty to a rightful ruler. Go now, and who is there to whom we can pay our homage? Who will stand with unquestionable right at the head of this realm?"

Robert stood silent for a moment, gazing at the face of one and then of another. Through the minds of at least three of those present flashed the thought: "I am closely akin. I have the right to rule in his place—and I will."

Silently the duke looked at them. Then, still without a word, he unsheathed his sword and beat with the hilt sharply three times upon the heavy table before him. What did it mean? It was mysterious, and in those days whatever was a mystery was expected to be of satanic origin. What evil spirits might come forth at the magic call? Those brave fighters gazed into Robert's face as if spellbound. They actually feared. He was called "Robert the Devil." Would he make good his name?

The curtain was drawn aside, and there stepped forward into the council room a handsome boy of seven years. He was dressed in a tunic of the richest, softest silk, falling to the knees. It was of a deep blue, and all around its lower edge and about the opening at the neck there was a wide border of elaborate silken embroidery, with a pearl gleaming here and there among the brilliant colors. No thought of fear had the child. He stood for a moment looking about the room. Then when he saw the duke, he went quietly to him and said:—

"Father, the chamberlain said that you wanted me."

"I do, and the man here that does not want you is an unfaithful vassal, and on him will I wreak my vengeance." He held the boy up in his arms and kissed him before them all. Then he said:—

"If any one among you dares to say that I am leaving you without a head, let him come forth. This child is my son. That he is the offspring of a peasant mother matters naught to you. Look at him; will he not be a fit man to represent you at court, to lead you in battle, and to render you justice? He is little, but he will grow. He is beautiful, gallant, and brave. I name him as my heir, and I here give him possession of the duchy of Normandy. From this moment he is your liege lord. Refuse to acknowledge him, if you wish to meet the penalty that is inflicted upon a faithless vassal."

The whole assemblage was so taken by surprise that not a word was spoken. The duke waited for a moment, then he turned to Alain of Brittany.

"Alain of Brittany, my cousin, *my friend*," he said significantly, "to you I intrust my son's possessions. I appoint you governor of Normandy until I return; and if I do not return, then are you governor until my boy is of age to rule his own domain. Do you accept the trust?"

"I do," said Alain gravely.

"Is there any one here who has aught of objection to bring forward?" asked the duke. He would have been a bold man who dared to brave the will of "Robert the Devil" to his face, and not a word was said. There was another reason for the silence. Alain was the strongest of the three that had had some hope of the kingdom, and his voice was hushed by the dignity offered him as governor of Normandy for, it might be, many years; and, moreover, although the charge of the interests of a tanner's grandchild and the maintenance of his rights would be at best no easy and no welcome task, he felt himself in honor bound to grant, for the sake of his promised friendship, what the duke had asked of him.

As for the others, they knew well that the first claim set forth by any one of them would be the signal for determined opposition on the part of the rest. There had been no opportunity to gain any man's support by bribes or promises or threats. No man present knew what allies he could count upon. The result of it was that one by one the bishops, archbishops, barons, and all the haughty company of nobles meekly folded their hands, hardened by the grasp of the sword and browned by the sun of many battlefields, and laid them, within the hands of the tanner's grandchild, and promised to be faithful to him as their feudal chief.

During the long, tiresome ceremonial the little boy was perfectly composed. He had more than once seen a vassal do homage to his father, and he felt a manly pride in behaving just as he had seen his father behave on similar occasions. There was something more. There had been little slights and rebuffs on the part of the nobles, and there had been words whose meaning he did not know, but with a child's quick sensitiveness he had felt that the nobles were not his friends, and it is no wonder that he had an instinctive pleasure in seeing them bow down before him. He might well sit quietly and receive with a certain childish dignity their oaths of fealty.

"If I were the Duke of Normandy, I would not leave a boy like that so that every one who wanted the dukedom might strike a blow at him," said one noble, as they went out from the council chamber.

"What can he do?" said another. "Who knows what sins Robert the Devil may have to answer for? It may be no wonder that he wants to go on a pilgrimage."

"No one would think that the mother of that boy was a peasant," said the first.

"The duke never seems to think of it, either. The child is his, and that is enough in his mind. He does not seem to remember that the blood of the tanner's daughter flows in the veins of the boy," said the other.

It is enough to make one think he is right to look at that child. I don't believe there is another boy in Normandy as brave and as handsome as he. They say it is really a pretty sight to watch him train that little company of youngsters. I suppose you heard about his leading them up to his father's castle and calling on the duke to surrender?"

"No, but I did hear that when he was playing one day on the bank of the Ante below the castle, a much larger boy than he came up behind him and whispered, 'This is where your father first met Arletta.' The little fellow understood somehow that it was an insult to his mother, and they say that the small child whirled around, and in the wink of an eye the other boy was in the water, for the blow was so sudden that he had no idea what was coming. Then the seven-year-old baby took his sister by the hand and walked off, never looking over his shoulder, and with his head high up in the air, just exactly as the duke carries his."

"It's a fine thing to be governor of Normandy," said the first, after a moment's pause; "but for all that, I don't envy Alain of Brittany."

"No one but Duke Robert would have thought of making him the child's guardian, a man whom he had just pursued almost to the death."

"What will you wager that he will be faithful?"

"I'll wager my castle that he will have a hard time of it if Duke Robert isn't at home within a year, and that either the child or Alain will suddenly die. Did you see the face of William of Montgomery? I did, and if he does not mean mischief, I am no prophet."

"The duke has been generous with him."

"What is, hold fast; what is to come, be grateful for; what is past, forget. That's William's way of doing it."

The feudal system was a great chain. Each one of those who had sworn to be true to the child William had received promises of fealty from men who paid him dues and were dependent upon him for protection. Now William, in his turn, must pay his homage to the king.

Robert had made most careful provision for Arletta, and as the grand procession swept away from Falaise one bright morning, she watched it, with her little daughter Adelaide, from a window that was hung with the richest draperies. Grieving to lose her son, she was nevertheless greatly comforted by the thought that it was *her* son for whose sake all this splendid cavalcade was marching to Paris. Moreover, this separation was to her almost a mark of nobility, for while peasant mothers might keep their boys, the sons of nobles were taken from them at the age of seven and put under the care of men, either at home or in some friendly castle, that they might the sooner learn the duties of knighthood.

King Henry was glad of the opportunity to appear grateful to Duke Robert for the assistance that he had rendered in his time of need, and the special court which he held to receive the Normans was most magnificent. The king sat on his royal throne. His velvet mantle glittered with gold and was loaded with ermine. Upon his head rested his jewelled crown. Barons, bishops, archbishops, and officers of state were around him, each in his most gorgeous array.

When the ducal party appeared, the dazzling company separated to the right and to the left, leaving a broad aisle from the entrance up the long hall to the foot of the throne. Slowly the duke and his men walked between the glittering lines, the duke leading his child. The boy's tunic was of a deep crimson velvet, the richest that Italian skill could produce, but with no touch of ornament. Beside him was the duke, barefooted, bare-headed, and wearing the coarse gray cloak that marked him as one who would make the great pilgrimage. His haughty bearing, not to be disguised even by the garb of the pilgrim, together with the beauty and animation of the boy, held every eye.

They knelt at the foot of the throne, and King Henry gave Robert a most gracious welcome. The duke then formally presented William as his son and heir, and said to the king:—

"King Henry, my liege, now that I am on the point of departing on a holy pilgrimage for the good of my soul and the forgiveness of my sins, I have brought to you my son, to whom I have given my duchy, and I ask that you will graciously receive his promise of fealty." Then said the king:—

"I will receive it, and I will do all that can fall to the share of him who is as faithful to his vassal as he would have the vassal be to his lord." Then the little boy knelt again before the throne. He folded his hands and laid them within the hands of the king. Phrase by phrase he repeated after his father:—

"I do now swear that from this day forth I will be your man, that I will serve you with life and limb and worldly honor, and that I will keep my faith and be loyal to you forever." Then the king said:—

"I do now accept you as my true and honest vassal. I will protect your person and your estate; and all things that a lord should perform for his faithful vassal, those will I do for you." The king then kissed the boy and gave him a green twig and a bit of turf, for in these feudal relations people had a theory that all the land belonged to the king, and that in return for the promised service of the vassal, he would allow him to make use of a certain amount of it; and it was this privilege which was signified by the presentation of the twig and the turf.

Now things became less formal. Cupfuls of silver coins were scattered among the poor people, and the king and all the nobles partook of a great feast. King Henry was most cordial to the duke, and especially attentive to his little new vassal. He promised that the boy should have a home at his own court, and there be trained in all such exercises of chivalry as were fitting to be taught to the future ruler of a great duchy like Normandy.

"You must grow fast, my little man," said one of the French nobles to William, "for there isn't a handsomer knight in King Henry's court than you will be."

"Will the king let me be a knight very soon?" asked the child eagerly. "I'm a pretty big boy now."

"Judging from the way he behaves, he will do whatever you wish," said the noble, with a meaning glance at another who stood near him.

"What does that look signify?" asked the other, with a little smile, as the boy wandered away to look at the pictures on the tapestry.

"Need it signify anything?" asked the first.

"Even looks are not without meaning when one dwells in a royal palace," said the other. "Do you mean that King Henry will not always be as devoted to the interests of his young vassal as he seems to-day?"

"Who shall say?" answered the first, with a shrug of the shoulders. "Normandy is a fair country. It joins France; there would be no opposition on this side."

"Do you not incline to think that Alain of Brittany will keep faith with Robert?"

"Who knows?" said the first, with another shrug; "but even if he does, there is William of Montgomery and the Archbishop of Rouen. More than one man, more than two, more than three, would be willing to accept the fertile lands and the flourishing manufactories of Normandy. Who knows what will happen?"

"Who knows?" said his companion.

CHAPTER V

THE LITTLE DUKE

I N spite of King Henry's urgent hospitality, Duke Robert was much too eager to be on his way to Rome to linger for many days in the French court, and before a week had passed he had begun his journey.

It was a great company. Many of Robert's nobles accompanied him, among them Drogo, count of his new possession, the Vexin, and Toustain, his chamberlain and favorite attendant. Not all of these travellers went necessarily for the good of their souls and the forgiveness of their sins, as Robert put it; some went because a pilgrimage was an exceedingly interesting expedition. No one knew what perils might be met by the way, and the flavor of danger gave an added zest to the enjoyment of seeing new countries and journeying in unknown places. Moreover, to have gone on a pilgrimage was with many people a strong title to a peculiar respect and deference that could be gained in no other way. There was another advantage, though perhaps no one counted upon it in setting out—the memory of such a journey, combined with a little imagination, would provide a man with enough materials for story-telling to the circle around his hall fire for all the rest of his life.

There was a long train of servants and attendants. The men that cared for the horses would make quite a troop by themselves, for there must be war-horses, in case any fighting was necessary; and there must be pleasure-horses, for every once in a while Robert would forget that he was a humble pilgrim, and then the whole party would canter along the way as merrily as if they were on a pleasure trip instead of a pilgrimage. There must be many beasts of burden, and their load was by no means light, for they bore the provisions for man and horse, and all the other necessities for the journey. Many of the pack-horses were loaded with skins filled with wine, sewn up and coated thickly with pitch. There were harbingers, of course, whose special duty it was to ride in advance of the rest of the company and arrange for lodgings and entertainment wherever they could be had; but such places were few, and it was desirable that the pilgrims should be able to stop to rest wherever they might choose.

Through France they went, through Switzerland,—or rather, what are now France and Switzerland,—over the Alps, and into Rome. So far the duke was a pilgrim,—when he did not forget it,—but on leaving Rome he became a mere traveller, and set out for Constantinople, and then for the Holy Land. Frequent tidings came by messenger to the little boy at the French court. One man reported the duke's great humility, and said that when a warder struck him with his staff and told him not to loiter by the way, Robert bore the blow meekly, saying that it was the duty of pilgrims to suffer.

Then came another tale of his prank in Rome, where he threw a rich mantle over the shoulders of a statue of the Emperor Constantine, "to protect him from the wind and cold," said this merry pilgrim.

The Norman notion of a jest was not exactly in accordance with modern ideas, and the Normans seem to have found it exceedingly amusing that when in Constantinople the duke entered the handsome audience chamber of the Emperor of the East he rolled up his embroidered cloak, dropped it on the floor, and made a seat of it, refusing to take it when he left, because it was "not the custom of the Normans to carry their seats away with them." Equally entertaining they thought the speech of Robert when a Norman on his homeward way saw him borne in a litter by four black slaves, and asked the duke what message he would send to Normandy. "Tell them," said Robert, "that you saw four demons bearing me to Paradise."

Everywhere he lavished great sums of money. He was Robert the Magnificent wherever he went, and often Robert the Reckless. The story is that in entering Constantinople he had his horse shod with shoes of silver. They were but slightly nailed on, so that they might drop off by the way and be picked up by whosoever would. At Jerusalem he made a better use of his wealth by paying for the great numbers of needy pilgrims outside the city the golden bezant demanded of each of them before they were allowed to enter.

Robert was wildly extravagant in his expenditures, and also in his penances, but it was an extravagant age. The scenes of remorse were as theatrical as the scenes of crime were tragic. Only a few years before Robert's pilgrimage, Foulques Nerra, Count of Anjou, made three journeys to the Holy Land, and once on reaching Jerusalem he had himself bound to a hurdle and dragged through the streets of the city, while by his own orders two of his servants scourged him most unmercifully amidst his cries of "Have pity, O Lord, have pity!" Robert's excesses were no greater than those of his contemporaries, and there seems no reason for the story that arose that he was insane.

Before many months had passed, a sad message came to the little boy at the French court, for Robert had died at Nicæa, by poison, it was thought. As a mark of special honor, permission was given that he should be buried in the Byzantine basilica of Saint Mary.

"It is the beginning of troubles," said Alain of Brittany to himself, and he set out to have an interview with William. "Much depends upon what kind of boy he is," thought Alain, "and a year may have changed him greatly."

The change had indeed been great, and in Alain's eyes it was for the better in every respect. The boy had grown tall and large, and had a manly bearing, which pleased the governor of Normandy.

"Do you know what you are to be when you grow up?" asked Alain.

"Yes," said the boy. "My father was Duke of Normandy, and that is what I am to be."

"And supposing that there are people who will try to keep you from being duke?" said Alain, to see what the boy would say.

"But I *am* the duke," said William. "No one can keep me from it."

"And what will you do if they take your castles?"

"I shall say, 'This is my castle, and you must give it up.' "

"And what will you say if they do not give it up?"

"Then I shall not say anything to the people in my castle, but I shall say to my men: 'Bring up the arbalests, tear down the walls, put up the scaling ladders;' and I shall go first, and I shall say: 'Come on, my men, follow me; rally round my gonfalon; strike with your swords. This is my castle, and no one shall keep it away from me.' " The boy drew himself up to his full height. His cheeks blazed and his eyes flashed as he paced quickly up and down the room, now thrusting an imaginary lance, and now drawing an imaginary sword.

"There's not another child like him in France," thought Alain. "He's not much more than eight years old, and he looks as if he were twelve. He's a fine boy, and he shall have his duchy, if there's any power in my right hand to—"

"Why did you put your hand on your sword?" asked William.

"In these times one must remember where his sword is," said Alain. The boy was silent for a moment; then he said:—

"I have a sword, and it is larger than the one that I used to have, because I am a bigger boy. If I am Duke of Normandy, when shall I be big enough to go to Falaise? Isn't that my castle?"

"I believe you captured it," said Alain with a smile. William looked abashed.

"I was only a little boy then," he said. "I should know better now; but I mean, shall I have to grow much taller before I am a real duke? I'm stronger than any other boy of my age—not one of them can bend my bow—and I can throw a spear and ride a horse— my father said perhaps I might go to fight when I could ride a horse—and I can wear heavier armor than any other boy at the court. What shall I have to do before I go to Normandy?"

"Perhaps we shall ask you to go to Normandy very soon," said Alain, "if King Henry is willing."

"Did my father have to ask King Henry if he might go to his castle?" asked the boy.

"No," said Alain with a little smile, "King Henry asked your father for permission to go to his own; and when you are grown up, I think it will be you to whom people will come to ask what they may do. But tell me, would you be afraid to go where men were trying to take your castles and to kill you?"

HE RODE THROUGH THE CASTLE GATE

"No," said the boy simply. "There were people who tried to kill my father, and he wasn't afraid; but where is my mother, and where is Adelaide? Now that my father is dead, I want to take care of them."

"And so you shall when you are older," said Alain; "but they are in a safe castle, and strong men are guarding them."

"I shall be a strong man soon;" said William, drawing himself up, "and I shall learn all there is to know about fighting. Thorold is teaching me. I like Thorold. He taught me how to ride, and King Henry hasn't a horse that can throw me. Could my father ride better than that?"

Soon Alain took his farewell, and went away.

"He's a brave boy," he said to himself, as he rode through the castle gate. "I almost wish he was in Normandy, and yet, perhaps King Henry is right in keeping him here. He might be murdered in a day."

And indeed, there was murder and robbery and devastation in every corner of Normandy. People believed that as soon as a king was dead, whatever laws he had made ceased to be of force, and that any promises that they had made to him were no longer binding; and so between the death of a king and the proclamation of what was called the "king's peace,"—a peace which was not peace at all, unless it was accompanied by an enforcement of the claims of the next heir as king,—every man did what he chose, and most of the nobles thought that such a break was the proper time to revenge themselves on their enemies, a time for burning and pillage and murder.

So it was in Normandy, as soon as it was known that the duke was dead. The nobles who made promises to serve him if he would protect them, now said that there was no one to protect them, and so they were freed from all service. William was proclaimed duke. "But what does that amount to?" said the nobles scornfully. "He is only a child. A child cannot see to it that we have justice done us, and he cannot lead us in battle. We want a strong man for our duke—and we do *not* want the grandson of a tanner."

There was no very definite law of succession to the dukedom, and if Robert had left a grown-up brother, or if there had been any one person with a good claim to the duchy on whom the nobles could unite, the little boy at King Henry's court would have had small chance of ever becoming the ruler of Normandy, even if he could ride any horse in the royal stables; but the difficulty was that there were so many people who thought that the boy's inheritance ought to be theirs. Rollo, the Norman chieftain, who had been the first duke of Normandy, had left many descendants, and every one of these was sure that no one else had so good a right to rule the land as himself. There were six of these relatives whose claims had some shadow of justice; but of the six, one was a monk, one a priest, and one an archbishop. Of the other three, one was Alain of Brittany, who held himself in honor bound to save for the child the lands that had been intrusted to him; another was William, Count of Arques, a half-brother of Duke Robert; and the third was Guy of Burgundy, a nephew of Robert.

There was another reason for the turbulence in the duchy. No one was allowed to build a castle without the permission of the ruler of the country; but in Robert's time he had been so sure that he could put down any uprising, that he had made no objection to the erection of a castle wherever any one chose to put one. Now very few of these strongholds were at all like what we should call a castle to-day. Not all of them were of stone, by any means. Even a square wooden tower with a moat and a drawbridge was called a castle; but in the three districts of Normandy in which the greatest number of fighters lived there were at least one hundred and thirty-two built so solidly that even now their remains may be seen. Every noble who had built a castle stood by himself, and in spite of what they had said, these men were not at all eager to have a strong man become duke and limit their independence. So it was that, instead of uniting at once to revolt against William, they all revolted against one another, and against all law and order. Every man did just as he chose, and many chose to avenge any wrongs that they fancied had been done them. Robbery and fire and murder were in every corner of Normandy. Nothing could quiet the disorder but a duke who ruled either by undisputed right or by irresistible force.

William was only a child, but he had one great advantage—his guardians were true to him and to his interests. One guardian has already been mentioned, the brave Alain of Brittany, whose special care was that the duchy of Normandy should be held for Robert's son. The second was the old soldier Thorold. The third was Seneschal Osbern, and the fourth was Count

Gilbert of Eu. King Henry was a kind of overlord to these men, and the boy was still at his court.

There were others whose friendliness to William was of the greatest value, those men who had gone on the pilgrimage with Robert, and who were now beginning to return to Normandy. They brought with them the relics of saints and martyrs that Robert had collected in the east, and had intrusted to his chamberlain Toustain to present to the Abbey of Cérisy. Robert had founded this abbey not long before he went on his pilgrimage, and he had expected to be buried within its walls. He had endowed it richly, but no more valuable gift could he have bestowed upon it than those bits of hair and bone and wood, those fragments of gowns and scourges and psalters; for men who came to look upon them never failed to leave a generous offering in the fortunate church to whose care they had been intrusted. Few of these visitors went away without a thought of Duke Robert and some gain of friendliness toward the little boy whom he had loved so well. As for the travellers themselves, people thought of them with a sincere reverence, because they had been pilgrims. Then they remembered that Robert, too, had been a pilgrim, and many of them began to feel that the child whom he had left in their care was fairly entitled to their loyalty. Moreover, these pilgrims had been chosen friends of Robert's, and their support of his child was worth much. All these strong allies of William were called together by Alain.

"I have asked you to meet," he said, "to decide whether it is best for the young duke to remain in Paris or to return to Normandy." Then said one of the councillors:—

"The duke is far safer in Paris than he would be here."

"Surely," said another, "there are enough who are loyal to defend a child and a castle."

"Yes, we can fight armed forces," said the first, "but can we fight poison or assassination?"

"There is another side," said one who until then had been silent. "Soldiers need a gonfalon to rally about; so do our nobles of Normandy need to see the duke. They think of him as a child in the French court. Let them see him for themselves, a bold, brave, handsome boy on his own rightful heritage, and I believe that they will be far more likely to stand by him."

"Still, there is the danger," said the first that had spoken.

"Yes," said the silent one; "but shall we save the child and leave him a beggar, or shall we let him share the risk, that we may help him to hold fast to that which is of right his own?"

"Moreover," said another, "are we so sure that he is safe in Paris? King Henry owed his throne to Duke Robert, but France would not be unwilling to possess Normandy and the Norman sea-coast. A child's life is a small matter when one wants a kingdom. A child may easily die or disappear. There would be no other claimant on whom so many would unite, and in the tumult and confusion Normandy could easily be made a part of France."

Finally it was decided that William should be taken to Vaudreuil, the castle that Robert had recommended as a safe place for the boy. It was situated on an island in the river Eure, and a river would be a better protection than a moat. Moreover, it was in the district of Evreux in Normandy, and yet not too far from the French domain to call upon King Henry in case of need; for after all, no one could believe that he would forget what was due to the son of the man who had befriended him in the days when he most needed a friend.

First, however, the king's permission to remove the boy to Vaudreuil must be gained. The councillors had looked upon this as hardly more than a matter of form, but much to their surprise King Henry began to make objections; the boy was safer with him, he said; a removal would interfere with his military education, etc.

The councillors became a little alarmed when the escort returned without the young duke. They had thought of King Henry as of one upon whom they might call for aid. Was it possible that he really had plans against the boy and his heritage? Shut up in one of Henry's strong castles, he might be held all his life as a captive; and then there were a hundred means by which a child that was in the way might be disposed of, and no one be the wiser. A second escort was sent with more emphatic demands than the first, and after some delay, the king yielded. Thorold was appointed to take command of the escorting party. It was an unfortunate journey for him, for soon after reaching

Vaudreuil he was murdered by some unknown assassin.

It was a hard life for a boy in the stern, gray castle on the island.

"Why cannot my mother and Adelaide live with me?" the boy demanded. The guardians had thought it best that Arletta should be kept away from her son, so that the people might remember only that he was the child of Duke Robert, but they said:—

"You know that you are to be a great soldier, and a soldier must learn of men, not of women."

"But a soldier must take care of women," said the boy. His guardians made no reply, but before long they told him that his mother had married a loyal knight, Herlwin of Conteville, and that Adelaide was safe in their care.

"I wanted to take care of them myself," said the boy soberly.

"Some day you will be able to," said his guardians.

Meanwhile it was all that they could do to take care of him. Not a moment, night or day, could he be left alone; for, although they could perhaps prepare for an armed attack, who could tell when an assassin might steal into the stronghold? Who could be sure that the members of the young duke's own train were faithful? A strong hand laid upon the boy's throat, a drop of poison forced gently between his lips as he slept, and Normandy would be the helpless prey of him who might have the power to take it. Gilbert, Count of Eu, had already been murdered, and the faithful Alain of Brittany had been poisoned as he was besieging the castle of William of Montgomery. Who knew when a like fate would befall the young duke?

Osbern slept in the boy's room at night, and watched him by day as he would watch some precious jewel. Walter, his mother's brother, was always on guard; but in spite of all their vigilance, there came a terrible night when William of Montgomery and his men forced their way into the castle, coming so suddenly and so powerfully that even before an alarm could be made, the faithful Osbern was stabbed as he lay asleep in the bed beside the duke. In the darkness the murderers believed that they had slain the duke himself, and while they were rejoicing, Walter hid the boy and carried him away to safety; not to some stone castle, but to the cottages of the poor, where no one would think of looking for him.

This was only one of the many attempts that were made to kill William, and only one of the many times that he was rescued by the bravery and quickness of his uncle. When the castle failed, the cottage was always his refuge.

Every one of the men who had been chosen as guardians for William had been killed by the boy's enemies. Lawlessness was everywhere. If a man was not robbed, it was because he had nothing that was of value to his stronger neighbor; if he was not murdered, it was because his neighbor had nothing to gain by his death. To these robbers and murderers the fact that a son of their former duke was alive and among them was a continual threat of vengeance. If the boy could be killed, they were safe, they thought, from fear of punishment or interference. Thus far these men had triumphed. Would they continue to triumph?

CHAPTER VI

GUEST OR PRISONER?

A LL acts of William's protectors were done in his
name, and now messengers were sent to those of
the nobles who still wished for a united, peaceful
duchy to say that William, Duke of Normandy, had
called together his council. The first business was to
choose new guardians, and now the boy was of legal
age to have a voice in the matter.

Whether by his own wise instincts or by the advice of his council, his choice was Ralph of Wacey, the
son of that Archbishop of Rouen whom Duke Robert
had besieged in his castle at Evreu. Now Ralph had
been the murderer of Count Gilbert, but this appeal to
his honor conquered his hostility. He became military
tutor to William and commander-in-chief of the armies
of Normandy, and from that time he was one of the
boy-duke's strongest supporters.

Ralph ruled with a heavy hand. From one rebellious vassal to another he sped, ever leaving behind
him peace, and an obedience that, on the surface, at
least, bore every mark of loyalty. Under his firm, steady
control, the duchy might have become a land of law-
keepers instead of law breakers, had it not been for the

ruler of a neighboring domain who now began to lend a listening ear to all complaints that came from the treacherous nobles that dwelt in Normandy. This ruler was King Henry of France. Not long after the election of Ralph as William's guardian, he sent a formal demand for the young duke to come to Evreux to do him homage. William's council straightway assembled to consider the matter.

"Never has there been such a going to and fro between Paris and every part of Normandy as of late," said one of the councillors significantly.

"You mean by that that King Henry is a friend to Norman traitors?" asked another bluntly.

"That is a thing which I would not say," said the first; "but I hardly think he has forgotten that Normandy was once a part of the land of the Franks, and that his own capital stands on a river that is controlled by another power."

"For three generations the kings of France have owed much to the dukes of Normandy," said another, "and save for Duke Robert, King Henry would have been no king."

"King Henry said, 'I thank you,' and gave the duke the Vexin," said a fourth; "but that is past. Perhaps he would be willing to let Normandy keep the thanks, if he could take back the Vexin."

"Perhaps he would like also the Norman sea-coast. Perhaps he would like to have Rouen a French city once more," said another.

"I think he would," said gravely the one that had first spoken. "But the question just now is whether the duke shall be advised to go to Evreux to pay homage to the king. I admit that I do not like the place. To leave the stronghold of Vaudreuil—and go nearer the French capital seems to be full of danger."

"The duke could have a large train of attendants," said one, "and every one of them should be armed from head to foot. To refuse to pay homage would be to plunge the land into war with France. Just now the friends of the duke seem to be in power, but not every one who bends the knee is faithful. There may be many a traitor among those who seem to be truest. A refusal to pay homage may be only the pretext for which the king is waiting."

"A king who would seize upon a second kingdom would wait for no—" began one, but stopped; for the duke, who had been listening closely to every word, had risen to speak.

He was only a boy of twelve years, but most of them had been spent among grave, stern warriors. Hardly an hour of his life had been free from danger. Many a time he had listened to his guardians while they discussed in which place there was least chance of his being murdered, and whether some knight who had seemed to be loyalty itself was more likely to stand by him or to attempt to kill him. He had learned of arms and warfare, understanding perfectly that some failure to know how to defend a stronghold might lose him a castle, that some slight lack of skill in arms might cost him his life. Hawking and hunting had been almost his only recreations, and even in the hunting-field there were many dangers for one who threw himself into the chase with such headlong eagerness and delight.

One would not expect such a childhood to make a boy gentle and tender-hearted, but it could hardly fail to bring him to an early maturity, to make him bold and strong and hardy, and to give him coolness and judgment far beyond his years. This was why, when the young duke arose to speak, his council turned toward him, not with the mere polite attention of vassals to their feudal chief, not even with a keen curiosity to see what a boy of his age would say, but with much the same kind of consideration that they would have shown to the expression of opinion of a man of twice his years.

It hardly seemed possible that he was but a boy of twelve, so dignified and composed did he seem. He was tall and strong and well developed, and more than one of the councillors before him said to himself, "If I were on a field of battle, I should rather have him for a friend than a foe." Quietly assuming that the final decision lay in his own hands, the boy said:—

I have listened to the advice of my councillors. Since I am the duke of Normandy, I must not fear danger, neither must I plunge my country into war with France. I will go to the king and I will say, 'King Henry, I am now fully twelve years of age, and I come to you not only to do homage to my liege lord, but to ask the honor of knighthood from the king of France.' "

"Never was there such wisdom in so young a head," said one councillor to another, as they went out of the room. "Boy as he is, he has cut the knot when we could not. However it may be about going to do homage whenever and wherever the king of France may ask it, a young noble may go to an older one and demand the blow of the sword that shall make him a knight, and for this he must go to whatever place the older shall name."

"Surely," said another; "and no train of attendants can be too long for a young duke who is on his way to receive the golden spurs."

"It shall be as splendid an escort as the Norman duchy can furnish," said the nobles; and forthwith each one of them called out every man who was a vassal to him and owed him military service, to come to the appointed place with as handsome an equipment as he could command. The duke was unarmed,—for a vassal must not appear in arms to do homage to his suzerain,—but every one else was in full armor.

The horses had been groomed until they fairly shone. The coats of mail and the bright shields and lances and helmets glittered in the sunshine as the brilliant company set out. William was at its head, carefully guarded by Ralph of Wacey and twenty of the strongest men and most experienced fighters. A little distance before the ducal line rode ten men as advance warders, for who could tell what danger might be lying in wait for the young man upon whom so much depended? The rear was as closely watched; for although their force was so strong that they needed to have little fear of a direct attack, who knew what treacherous foes might be about them ready to cut the duke from his defenders?

King Henry received the duke with calm courage, but glanced with a shade of annoyance, the nobles thought, at the great company of armed men.

"You come to a friendly court in full array, it seems," he said to the duke.

"I have many friends who wish to see me receive the golden spurs," said the young noble, and the king was silent. A messenger had been sent to King Henry long before the company set out to say to him that William would ask for knighthood, and so all things had been made ready. The ceremony of homage was short, and then came the preparations for receiving the accolade, and these were by no means short or simple.

Every part of the preliminary rites was full of significance. First came the bath followed by the white tunic to indicate the purity which was expected of every true knight. Over the white tunic was put a red robe to call to mind the blood that the knight must always be ready to shed in a righteous cause. Over the red robe was drawn a close black coat, that the knight might never forget that death will finally come to all men.

If this ceremony had taken place in France, William would have been required to fast for twenty-four hours, to spend a night alone in the church praying before the altar, to confess and receive absolution, to attend service in the church and listen to a sermon about his new life and its duties; but the Normans were much inclined to feel that knighthood was more closely connected with warriors than with priests, and so much of the usual religious ceremony was omitted.

The rite, however, took place in the church, and it is possible that William followed the French custom of advancing to the altar with his sword hanging by a scarf about his neck; and that the priest took it off, laid it upon the altar, and blessed it. William advanced to the king and knelt before him with hands clasped, and said:—

"I am come to you, King Henry of France, to ask that I may be armed as a knight, and that all forms may be fulfilled that are necessary to my having the right to serve and command in all ranks." The king asked:—

"To what purpose do you wish to become a knight? Is it because you seek to be rich, to take your ease, to be held in honor among men without doing that which shall make you deserving of honor?" Then William answered:—

"I do not seek to become a knight for any honor save that of punishing those who do evil, of protecting the innocent and avenging their wrongs, and of maintaining true religion. If I am admitted to the noble rank of knighthood, I will endeavor to perform its duties faithfully and well."

Then all the knights in their shining armor gathered about the young duke. Then, too, came the ladies of the court in their most brilliant attire, and together they put the young man's armor upon him, piece by piece; first the golden spurs, then the coat of mail, the cuirass, and last of all the sword. Then the ladies and the knights drew back, and William, glittering in his flashing steel, advanced to the king and again knelt before him. The king unsheathed his own sword, a sword that had been reddened by the blood of many battles, and gave the duke the accolade,—that is, three light blows on the shoulder or the nape of the neck,— saying:—

"In the name of God, Saint Michael, and Saint George, I dub thee knight. Be valiant, bold, and loyal."

Again the brilliant company gathered around him. The knights flashed their swords over their heads and embraced him and welcomed him among them. A helmet was brought him, and a horse was led up to the church door. The newly made knight sprang upon its back, disdaining to make use of the stirrups, and galloped back and forth, poising his lance and brandishing his sword. One of the old chroniclers says:—

"It was a sight both pleasant and terrible to see him guiding his horse's career, flashing with his sword, gleaming with his shield, and threatening with his casque and javelins."

After all this came a most elaborate feast, when every one drank to his health and every one rejoiced in his new honors. Generous gifts were made to the minstrels and to all that had helped to entertain the guests; and finally large sums of money were distributed among the servants, that every one, even the humblest, might be glad in the young knight's gladness.

The homage was performed, the ceremony of knighthood was completed, the pleasures of the feast and the rejoicing were at an end, the formal farewell had been said, and the Normans prepared to set out on their homeward march to Falaise. William was about to mount his horse, when a chamberlain from King Henry stood before him, saying:—

"I am the bearer of a message from the king. It is this: 'King Henry of France, suzerain of the duchy of Normandy, summons his vassal, William, Duke of Normandy, to appear before him.'" The faces of the Normans were grave, but William still looked upon the king as the guardian whom his father had chosen, and without hesitation he advanced with only a small bodyguard to the royal audience chamber. The king gave him no word of greeting, but looked at him sternly and said:—

"I am little pleased, my young sir knight, with the reports that have come to me in regard to this new fort of yours at Tillières."

"My councillors have told me," answered William, "that the fort at Tillières was built by Richard the Good, the father of my father."

"It matters not," said the king, with a frown, "the fort stands, and it is garrisoned, and its men are making continual incursions into my territory."

"If that is true," said William, "I am very sorry. I will send a messenger to the commander of the fort. If my men have made incursions into your lands, they

shall be punished, and there shall be no more annoyance."

" 'No more annoyance!' " repeated the king an-
grily, "and 'If it is true!' I tell you, young sir, a vassal is
not to arm himself against his suzerain. The fort at Tillières is a menace and a threat, and it must fall; and until it falls, I look upon you as a rebellious vassal.
Perchance your councillors have told you how a rebellious vassal is to be treated." The king spoke harshly,
and sat gazing with the utmost sternness at the young
duke.

Mature as he was by reason of his bitter experience, William was but a boy after all, and in such a
strait as this even an older and wiser head might well
have been puzzled. He was silent.

"You cannot speak?" said the king. "Then I will
provide one that can speak for you. A messenger is in
readiness to bear to the commander of the fort at Tillières your orders that it be razed to the ground."

What could the boy do? He was in the hands of
the king, practically a prisoner at his court. Then, too,
he had spent many months in Henry's care, and he was
accustomed to obey him as he would obey a father.
There was no opportunity to consult his councillors;
he must decide the matter himself.

"Here is a scribe," said the king. "Will you send
to the governor of the fort an order to raze it to the
ground, and will you seal the order with your seal?"

"I will," said William slowly.

"I give you most courteous invitation to remain as my guest until word shall come that the castle of Tillières has been levelled," said the king ironically, and William was immediately escorted with a guard to a part of the castle from which it would have been almost impossible for his own men to reach him or for him to escape.

The order was sealed with the duke's seal and sent to the governor of the fort; but this independent governor calmly refused to surrender. He returned a brief message that the fort had been intrusted to him by Robert, duke of Normandy, to watch and ward as the heritage of his son William. It was impossible, he said, that this son should have given the order to destroy it, and he would surrender it to no one but the duke himself in person.

The king was more angry than ever, and now he sent a great armed force to tear down the castle. He expected that the sight of his soldiers would be enough to make the governor submit, but Gilbert Crispin was made of somewhat unyielding material. He shut himself up in the castle with his men, and there he stayed. Henry's soldiers attacked the fort, and the governor was more determined than ever when among them he recognized some of the traitorous Norman nobles, who either preferred to pay their allegiance to a suzerain that would be chiefly in another district, or who were eager to help on any kind of warfare that they might the more readily find opportunities for robbery and pillage.

Gilbert's reply to the king's messenger had left it to be inferred that if the duke himself in person commanded him to give up the fort, he would yield; but when King Henry in a storm of anger had William taken to Tillières, even then, with the duke before him, Gilbert hesitated, and it was only when the orders of the duke were seconded by those of the council that he submitted. The gates were thrown open, and the faithful governor and his valiant men marched out. The castle was in the hands of the French, and they at once set fire to it. The roofs and floors were burned, and the stone tower, blackened and despoiled, stood as a gloomy monument to the unjust claims of the French king.

Again the council met, and now Henry was recognized as an undoubted foe.

"I am but young in knighthood," said William; "but when I received my arms, I was told that a true knight would never couch his lance against the noble who had given him the accolade. Shall I be true to my oath of knighthood, or shall I fight against my suzerain?"

"It is the duty of a knight to be faithful to him who has admitted him to knighthood," said one of the council, "and therefore as a loyal knight you cannot couch your lance against him; but you are more than a knight. King Henry is your feudal chief, and you are his vassal. You owe him service, and he owes you protection. If he has broken his promise of protection by himself invading your lands, you are no longer bound by your promise of service. As a knight you cannot fight him; but as the duke of Normandy you are bound to defend your country and protect it from every one that would work it harm."

It was evident enough that King Henry intended to work it harm. He seemed to have forgotten that the duke was his ward, and that by every tie of honor he was bound to be faithful to the boy's interests. Apparently he had no recollection of the fact that, save for the aid of William's father, he would have had no power to harass the son.

Henry began to march his forces into the district beyond Tillières, and now the Norman council realized that by surrendering the fort at the king's demand, they had only weakened themselves without lessening his longing for the broad and fertile lands of Normandy. Faster and faster came the bands of Frenchmen into the Norman boundaries, each company venturing farther than those that had preceded it. Into the very centre of the Norman domain they pushed their way.

If all Normandy had been faithful to William, there would have been little chance for the ravages of any foreign power; but some preferred the tumults of war to the restraints of peace, some blamed the duke, boy as he was, for the loss of the fort of Tillières, and there were many among the proud nobles of Normandy who still declared that they would never submit to the "grandson of a tanner."

Even in the district of the Hiesmois, it was not difficult to find a traitor. In the very heart of Falaise, in the castle itself, was the man whom the council had trusted, and whom the bribes and promises of Henry now succeeded in making unfaithful to his trust. This traitor, governor of the castle, rid himself one by one of the soldiers who would have stood by their duke, and garrisoned the castle with men from the forces of the French.

CHAPTER VII

"WILLIAM KNOWS HOW"

T HERE could hardly have been a heavier blow to
William than to find that the castle of his birth-
place, the home of his childish memories, was the very
centre of the attack upon him. It is no wonder that he
was aroused to a fury of indignation. He was no longer
alone, as he had been at King Henry's court when he
was forced to give up his border fort. He had by his
side a wise man, well skilled in the art of war, his
guardian, Ralph Wacey, and by his advice the duke
called out all the nobles who were faithful to him to
rally around his standard.

In the castle of Falaise was the traitor governor
with some few of William's friends who could not be
sent away without arousing suspicion, and as many of
Henry's men as could well be brought within its walls.
On three sides of the fort was the steep and rocky
precipice at whose foot clustered the houses of the
town. About the town was a wall, and beyond the wall
were encamped the forces of the French.

All was arranged. The French troops were to
make their way through the town, carry on a pretended
siege for a short time, and then the traitor within the

castle was to be false to his trust and surrender the fort to the soldiers of the king. Henry's commander outside the wall of the town had no thought of a surprise. The castle was sure, the people in the town would not dare to make any resistance, and there was little possibility of the duke's coming against them; so one morning they leisurely made ready to enter the town.

The leader had not yet fully armed himself for the fight when rapid hoofbeats were heard, and a horseman galloped at full speed into the royal camp. His horse was wet with sweat and covered thickly with dust and foam. The rider dropped from his saddle and fell on the ground at the feet of the commander. He tried in vain to speak, for his mouth was so parched and dry that he could not utter a word. With a great effort he pointed feebly down the road. Men brought water. They wiped away the stifling dust. They lifted him up. They poured wine down his throat. Again he pointed and whispered a single word. It was, "William!" and he fell back on the ground weak and help-less.

Now William had not so many men as the king, but every man was true and resolute. They fell like a storm-wind upon the French camp, and the king's troops fled for their lives. So far it was well for the Normans, but there were foes in the castle, William knew that; and how would it be with the town? From the lack of heavy engines of war in the abandoned French camp, the king's men evidently did not expect very much difficulty in entering the town. How would it be when the Normans should try to enter?

The time that he had to wait in uncertainty could almost be measured by minutes, for men on the walls had quickly recognized the young duke. He was their duke, and their home was his. He was coming to his own, and never did an heir come to his own with greater rejoicing.

"Welcome! Welcome!" they shouted. "Hail to the son of Arletta! Welcome!" Banners and strips of bright-colored cloth and green branches of trees were waved joyfully as the Norman forces entered the Norman town. Women held up their children to see the duke.

"That's he," they called, "on the black horse. Look at him! See how he rides! His father used to ride like that, and his mother was one of us, and he is our own duke. Look at him! Hail to the son of Arletta!" And one peasant woman, who was holding up her baby and who had nothing else to wave, actually waved the baby in her excitement as the duke rode by, and the baby's cries mingled with the cheers of the people.

Now ever since William was seven years old he had lived among stern warriors. They had taken care of him as a valuable piece of property, and they had guarded him from injury as they would have guarded a piece of property. He had trusted King Henry, and the king had met him with coldness and blame and imprisonment. Never before, since the death of his father, had the young duke received a sincere, hearty welcome. It is no wonder that ever after this day his love for the town below the precipice was firm and sure.

Through the familiar streets he rode at the head of the line. Past the river Ante they went, and his cheeks burned under the cold steel of his helmet as he remembered the insult of the boy whom he had pushed into the stream.

"Hail to our duke, the son of Arletta!" the people cried. And under the steel helmet the stern young duke smiled, and with fresh courage rode up the winding way to the castle. Not quite pleasing to the proud Norman nobles were these cries of "Arletta," but it was no time to be critical; friendly enthusiasm was worth more than pride just then.

"You have taken the castle once," said Ralph Wacey, who had heard of William's childish exploit, "and it ought to be easy to take it again."

"Easy or not easy, we will have it," said William, and in a moment his wrath came back at the thought that it was the castle of the town of Falaise, the castle of his own home, that had rebelled.

The attack was furious, and the defence desperate, for the faithless governor knew full well that death was the just penalty of such guilt as his. The Normans fought fiercely, but the castle was strong. Forenoon, afternoon, sunset,—still they fought, the attack as violent and the defence as obstinate as in the early morning. Just as darkness began to hide the assaulters from their foes within the castle, the duke's men succeeded in making a breach in the outer wall.

The false governor put up a white flag and begged for mercy. Few men would have refused to be merciful after such a victory and in the first great joy of their lives. William pardoned the traitor on condition of his leaving Normandy forever. The district which he had held as a vassal of the duke was, of course, taken from him; and a large share of this land, the first winnings of that sword which was to conquer wherever it was unsheathed, William immediately presented to the mother whom he had scarcely seen since the days of his early childhood in Falaise.

When Tillières was surrendered, one condition was that it should not be restored for four years; but King Henry, ever faithless, paid no heed to his promise, and soon the fort stood in all its early might, the stonework repaired and strengthened, the roofs and floors renewed; and now, instead of being a protection to Normandy, it was a constant threat of invasion and conquest.

In the middle of the eleventh century there seems to be nothing but fighting. The governments were weak; if men would protect their rights they must fight for them. It was not only one man and his retainers fighting against another man with the men whom he could bring into the field; in the chain of feudalism every man had sworn to give military service to some one of greater power than he, and every man had sworn to give protection to several men who were of less power than he. Whenever any link of the chain was touched, the whole chain quivered.

In those troublous times,—those days of destruction, rebellion, and the foulest of treachery,—the one power in the land was the church. The church cried "Peace," and peace there was to an extent that would have seemed impossible. Too wise to require what no fear of her thunders would force men to grant, the church limited her demand for peace to Sunday and the last three days of each week. During those days not a sword was to be unsheathed, not a blow struck. The clergy proclaimed:—

"It is the peace of God. Whoever shall break it, let him be accursed." Then they turned their lighted tapers downward and extinguished them, while the people chanted:—

"And so may God extinguish the joys of every one who shall refuse to observe peace and justice." Whoever broke this law was shut out of the church. If he died before bringing about a reconciliation, he was forbidden to receive Christian burial. The only way for him to win forgiveness was to confess his fault with all meekness, atone for whatever wrong he had done, leave home and friends, and spend many years of penance in exile.

With this law of the church and William's increasing power, the condition of Normandy became greatly improved. He offered free pardon to all who would lay down their arms, and gave generous rewards to those who were true to him. He was interested in commerce, he encouraged manufactures, he maintained peace with the neighboring states wherever peace was possible. His relations with King Henry of France were of the only character that could be wisely maintained with that changeable monarch; that is, he was on the terms of peace and allegiance that were proper between vassal and suzerain, but he did not neglect to make friends with those nobles especially who had some reason to dislike the king of France. After all the murders and revolts, there seemed to have come a time of peace. Even the duke might borrow a few days for rest and pleasure.

William and his court went to Valognes—"pleasant Valognes." Day after day they hunted in the forest and feasted at the castle. One night, after the guests had departed full of plans for the next day's hunt, the last day before the duke was to return to Rouen, William was so sound asleep that not even a loud knocking on the gate aroused him.

"Open, open!" a voice cried. "Enemies are coming, fly! Rise, wretches, you will all be murdered!"

"It's the duke's jester," said one of the household sleepily. "He's trying to play some trick on us. Go down and let him in. The duke will be angry if he is kept out all night." So the door was opened and the jester burst in.

"Where's my master?" he cried, "where's William? William, where are you?" and in spite of the half-laughing, half-sleepy attempts of the watchman to stop him, he made his way to the door of William's chamber and beat upon it madly.

"Master, master," he cried, "open the door, open it! They are coming to kill you! Fly, fly!"

"Who are you?" said William.

"Gallet, master, your own jester. I heard them at Bayeux. I slept in the stable and—" But William had thrown open his door, and there was a strange figure, for the jester wore a close-fitting doublet of red on the right side and yellow on the left. His right stocking was yellow and the left was red. Over his doublet was a coat of all the colors of the rainbow. A yellow hood covered his head, pointed, and with little bells hanging from every point. In his hand was a wand with what had been a fool's head, but now it was flattened and broken where its owner had beaten it against the door.

"Is this one of your pranks?" demanded the duke sternly.

"I heard them, indeed I did, and I saw the horses and the arms, and they are coming to kill you, and I love you, master, and if they come, you will never, never again see the light of day. Fly, master, fly!"

One glance at the face of the jester was enough. This was no untimely prank; it was fearful truth. William made the sign of the cross. He thrust on a tunic, buckled on a sword, caught up a travelling cloak and ran, barefooted and bareheaded, to the stables. He was only nineteen years of age, but he showed the wisdom of sixty, for he trusted no one. Whom could he trust in all his duchy but the poor jester? He saddled his horse and fled. From whom? To whom? Who could say?

The galloping of horses was heard, and it seemed but a moment before the castle was surrounded. Armed men swarmed from turret to dungeon. Where was William? The servants stood pale and trembling. They did not know, they said, and by their faces they told the truth. They clustered in a frightened group, terrified and silent. There was another group of the invaders, loud and angry, for the duke was nowhere to be found. Between these two groups, playing tricks on one man and then on another, was the jester. He was in high spirits. He tossed his stick with the broken fool's head. He whirled it around and around.

"One fool's head is broken," he said, "but the other fool's head is sound," and then he felt for the corners of his hood and shook his bells. "Too late, my brave men, too late," he cried, whirling around on the yellow foot and then on the red one, and turning somersaults in the very midst of the angry group. "William is gone. O William! Where's William? He'll make ready for you; William knows how. William knows, he does. You gave him a bad night, and he'll give you a bad day. How wise you are! Glad am I that I am a fool! William knows, he knows."

Now a jester might be tormented and he might be beaten, but no man cared really to injure one of these quick-witted, half-mad beings, for no one knew what evil might befall him who struck a deadly blow. So the jester jeered at them to his heart's content, but long before his antics were over, they were on their horses shouting:—

"Death to him! Death to him!"

Down the same road by which the traitors had come, William galloped. It was bright moonlight. The shadow of every rock and of every tree was black and dense. Who could tell behind which one an enemy might lurk, ready to spring out and strike the fatal blow? He heard horsemen coming furiously up the road. He slipped into the gloom of a thicket, and stood with his hands closely clasping his horse's nose, lest

DOWN THE SAME ROAD BY WHICH THE
TRAITORS HAD COME WILLIAM GALLOPED

the animal should neigh as the others came near. The horsemen dashed on. In their excited talk he was sure that he heard his own name. He was but a little way from the castle. His enemies would fail to find him, and then they would follow on his tracks. Not a moment could be lost. He thrust into his horse's sides the cruel Norman spurs that were fastened to the stirrups. The river Vire lay before him. If it was low tide, he could cross by the ford; if high, he must go far around. The tide was out, and he splashed through the shallow water in safety. Close by the shore on the opposite side stood the tiny stone church of Saint Clement, every line of it clear and distinct in the moonlight.

"God has helped me," said the fugitive. "To thank him cannot delay me." He sprang from his horse and burst into the little church. He threw himself before the altar. It was but a moment. On, on! they were pursuing. Bayeux lay before him, but—what was it that he had heard of Bayeux? Oh, the jester had said that his enemies were there. He must go north by lanes and by-paths between Bayeux and the sea; then he would pass Rye and come to the districts that he believed were faithful to him. The moon had long since set, but he had galloped on through the darkness. The east began to brighten. Here and there the sleepy twitter of a bird came from some tree above his head. Dew fell from the branches as he dashed by. There was a stone tower. Whose was it? No matter, every one was false; and once more the cruel spurs were plunged into the horse's bleeding sides.

All was quiet and peaceful in the castle. Hubert, its lord, stood just without the gate. Before him was the little church, and he was on his way to matins. He stopped a moment to look at the east, which was brightening with the rising sun. Then he turned to the west. He heard a furious galloping. What fugitive was this? No criminal must pass his castle gate. He sprang forward and caught the bridle rein. The horse was covered with foam and blood. On its back was a man without shoes or stockings, bareheaded, covered with dust. His mantle was torn to shreds by the briers through which he had come. His face was bleeding. He was clinging to his horse's neck, and as Hubert caught the bridle he sank to the ground. For a moment Hubert stood silent in amazement. Then he fell on his knees before the horseman.

"My duke, my duke," he cried, "what has happened? Where are your followers? Who has done this? Who pursues you? Trust me, and I will save you as I would save myself. Have I not sworn to be your loyal vassal, to be faithful to you as well as to God?"

"Many have sworn to be faithful," said William sadly, "but I trust you;" and then he told Hubert the story of the pursuit and the escape. They are on my track," he said; "I must flee."

"Then will I give you a guard," said Hubert, "and one that will not fail you." So Hubert brought him food and wine and clothes, and set the duke upon his own good horse.

"Fear not, my lord," said he; "the horse is strong and sure of foot, and he will hold out well to your journey's end." Then called he his three sons, three brave knights.

"Buckle on your swords, my three brave knights," said he, "for here is my lord and yours. Foul traitors have wished to murder him. Save him. Give your life for his, if need be. God gives glory and honor to him who dies for the lord to whom he has sworn to be faithful."

"We swear to be true to our own sovereign lord, Duke William of Normandy," said the three young men, making the sign of the cross. Then William and his guards left the sun on their left, and rode swiftly to the river Orne and crossed over, and soon the duke was safe in his own castle of Falaise.

Then was there great rejoicing, for the roads were full of peasants wandering to and fro, and saying with sadness and many tears, "Where is our duke? Is he a prisoner, is he wounded, or perchance is he slain? Who are the knaves that have done this?" And when they knew that he was neither a prisoner nor wounded nor slain, then were they joyful, and the heart of every one of them was glad.

But who were these foes that pursued William so savagely, and whose first move was an attempt at assassination? The leader was one Guy of Burgundy, his own cousin. Guy had spent much of his childhood at Falaise, and had received knighthood from William's hands. William had made him lord of two castles, and had treated him as if he was a younger brother. To this young man who had every reason for being loyal to his cousin, went one Grimbald, whose castle of Plessis was in the district of Bayeux.

"Did it ever enter your mind," said Grimbald, "that you are rightful heir to the dukedom of Normandy?"

"My father claimed no such right," said Guy, "and surely I have no claim that he had not."

"That is but a childish excuse," said Grimbald. "William's father had but a peasant wife. You are the lawful heir to the dukedom. You need only to stretch out your hand to take that which is your own. Do you not wish to be duke?" Then Guy began to wish for it, and soon he was sure that he had a right to the dukedom. All William's kindness was forgotten. From one noble to another this new claimant went. To the lords of the strong castles in western Normandy he said:—

"If I am duke, I shall content myself with the eastern part of the duchy, and you may go on building your castles and live in the independence which day by day you are losing under the rule of him who now unjustly holds control." Western Normandy stood by Guy, while eastern Normandy armed itself and was ready to fight to the death to maintain the rights of William.

The first act of the conspirators was the attempt to murder William which was frustrated by the devotion of the jester Gallet. Now the duke was in his castle. He knew who were false to him and who were true, but he had not the forces to conquer his foes. Whom should he ask? Up and down the room he paced. Suddenly he struck his hand on the hilt of his sword.

"I will do it," he said. "I do not bow down to one who has wronged me, I make him of service to me. I claim that which I have a right to claim, and if he gives it, it shall atone for the harm that he has done me." Straightway he started for the French court.

"To you as my suzerain I am come," he said. "You owe me protection. I am come to claim it. It was to you that my father, setting out on a holy pilgrimage, intrusted my interests. Had he done nothing to warrant him in his trust? Do you not hold your kingdom to-day because of the aid that he gave you? You came to him in your need with but twelve knights, and he treated you with honor and put you on the throne of France." Henry made no reply, and the duke went on:—

"The western districts will hold by my cousin. I can name you over the traitors one by one. You know well that not one of those men can unite Normandy or rule it if it is united, and you know that I can, if you help me to overcome these rebels." Still Henry was silent. Then said the duke:—

"It rests with you whether you will have Normandy united and under a strong hand, or whether you will have bloodshed and robbery and murder. Even if these men should ask to be your vassals, what kind of subjects, think you, will rebels and traitors become? Will they be any more true to you than they have been to me?" For the third time in William's few years of life, it had been shown that to throw one's self frankly upon the generosity of either Frenchman or Norman would often arouse in him a spirit of chivalry and honor. King Henry spoke at last.

CHAPTER VIII

A VISIT TO ENGLAND

"THE full truth has not been told me," he said. "And now that you have come directly to me to ask of your suzerain that which you have a right to ask, I will join you. I will lead my own troops in person, and I will put you on the ducal throne so firmly that no one shall ever dare attempt to thrust you from it. I came to your father with twelve knights, it is true, but I will come to you with three thousand, and with them shall come a great band of followers. This is what the king of France will do for his vassals."

So it was that William set out for what was to be one of the three decisive battles of his life. The hostile troops met at Val-ès-dunes, near Caen. The rebels came from the west; the French and the Normans from the east. As both parties were arranging their men, there came up from the south so noble a band that the leaders stopped, each hoping that these one hundred and forty knights, so finely armed and accoutred, would be on his side. Just between the opposing lines they came, and then halted as if to decide which to choose.

WILLIAM SETS OUT FOR BATTLE

"Who are they?" asked King Henry of William. "On whose side will they stand?"

"On mine, I think," said William, and he went up boldly to the leader.

"You are Ralph of Tesson," said he, "and when my father went to Jerusalem, you laid your hands in mine and swore to be faithful to me."

"And I have sworn also to be the first to give you a blow. I swore it on the shrine at Bayeux no longer ago than yestermorn."

"The French, the French, Ralph; go with the French," said the knights behind him softly. Ralph hesitated. "A man must keep his oath," he said, "and what's more, I will. Pardon me, my liege," said he, as he struck William lightly on the shoulder, "there's one oath kept; now come on, my men, for the other, and we'll stand by Duke William till the river runs uphill."

The two great bodies of knights rushed together, shouting their war-cries.

"Montjoie Saint Denis!" cried the French.

"God help us!" cried the Normans.

"Saint Amand! Saint Sever! Thury! Thury!" shouted the barons, making the hills resound with the names of their castles or their patron saints. Lances were shivered, shields were forgotten, and men fought hand-to-hand with swords, pikes—anything they could snatch up, even with their naked fists. King Henry was as eager to help William as he had been to harm him, and he flung himself into the wildest of the fight. A lance was thrust against him by a knight of the Cotentin district with such terrible force that he fell from his horse, and for many generations the minstrels of the Cotentin sang proudly:—

> "From Cotentin came forth the lance
> That once unhorsed the king of France."

But a Frenchman came to his aid, and the old chroniclers glory in the prowess of the king and in the victory of the young duke over the champion warrior of Bayeux.

The rebels retreated, but they escaped one death only to run into another; for over the steep river banks they were driven till the stream was red with their blood and the mill-wheels were stopped by their dead bodies.

What should be the punishment of the traitors, was the next question. Except on the battle-field, William almost invariably refused to take human life; so, although Guy still maintained his rebellion, and had to be besieged in his castle before he would yield, his life was spared. Even Grimbald,—the tempter and the would-be assassin, as it was proved,—even Grimbald was not put to death. After three years in prison, he died and was buried in his chains. On some of the conspirators, indeed, William did inflict a most useful and appropriate vengeance, and one not without a grim touch of humor; for he forced them to build a road from Valognes to Falaise, following closely the line of his mad gallop to save his life on the night of the attempted assassination.

Even after this victory, there were many disturbances which William had to suppress. Many a noble was still stung to the quick by the thought that he was forced to pay homage to a tanner's grandson. Many a knight, forbidden by his rank to engage in any pursuit except fighting, was ready to seize upon any pretext to take up arms. There were disturbances, but never again anything like a general revolt.

It was not long before William was called upon to help Henry in a war with Geoffrey, Count of Anjou. The district of Maine lay between France and Anjou, and the rulers of each country claimed it as tributary to himself. Just across the boundary and on the Norman side was the town of Alençon, the city of William Talvas of Belesme, who had cursed William when the duke was in his babyhood. On Norman ground as it was, this town had always hated the tanner's grandson, and the people gladly seized the opportunity to strike at him by aiding the count of Anjou. The soldiers of Anjou were welcomed into the town and formed a strong garrison for the fort.

Duke William was besieging another town some distance away, but he knew that if he struck at all, he must strike suddenly; so he marched all night, and just at sunrise drew up his men before Alençon. Soldiers were at the bridge, and a fierce reception they gave him. William fought with his usual vigor, but the men of Alençon were well armed and brave. They began to feel sure of the victory, and in their bravado they went one step too far. Not content with blows, they even ventured to enrage William with insulting words.

"Hail to the grandson of the tanner!" they shouted. Then they hung from the walls leather aprons and jerkins, and skins wet with blood and foulness, and called out:—

"Hides, hides, hides for the tanner! Plenty of work for the tanner! Come on, grandson of the tanner!"

Now from his earliest childhood, the least disrespect to his mother seemed to throw William into a passion that was almost like a fit of insanity. He had the one thought of revenge, and a terrible revenge he took. For one moment he stood still, then he swore a great oath that the men who had thus mocked him should be lopped off as are the branches of a tree. He fought like a very demon. The bridge was torn down; the palisades, the gates, the roofs of houses, everything that could be battered or burned, was destroyed. Still with grim, set face, William struck to the right, to the left. Lance or sword, it mattered not to him—the blow was all; and with every blow the tanner's grandson had one enemy the less.

Even then the castle refused to yield. William was beside himself with fury. He kept his fearful oath. The hands and feet of thirty-two of the men that had been captured were cut off, and with great slings they were flung over the castle wall. No wonder is it that at this ghastly threat the garrison surrendered, and begged most humbly for mercy. William had come to himself again, and he was merciful.

The one excuse that can be given for such savage barbarity is that it was the custom of the times.

While capital punishment was somewhat rare, men seemed never to hesitate to condemn a vanquished foe to lose eyes or limbs, or to be thrown into a dungeon so horrible that the life of a single day was worse than any death. Men seemed utterly without sympathy with the physical sufferings of others. Nearly forty years after the taking of Alençon, it was decreed by Henry IV, Emperor of Germany, that if a boy over twelve years of age offended against the truce of God by striking a blow that produced a wound, his hand should be stricken off.

William's devotion to his mother was shown in less violent ways than this, not only by his gifts to her directly, but by his watchfulness of the interests of his half-brothers. On one of them he bestowed the bishopric of Bayeux, and to the other he gave so large a grant of land as to place him at once among the principal landholders of Normandy. Neither bishop nor landholder could have been more than twelve years of age when the gift was made, but this, too, was done in accordance with the custom of the times; and it is the only instance in William's reign of his yielding to the old abuse of giving church positions to members of his family for whom he wished to provide.

Now that William had shown his ability to govern Normandy and to rule revolting vassals, his nobles became very anxious that he should marry. They had hope of a lasting peace under his strong control, if he only had a son to be his heir. The duke was now about twenty years of age. The chroniclers say that he was handsome, well formed, and far above the ordinary height of men. On more than one occasion he had

proved himself a man of bravery and power. His bravery would not diminish, and his power would increase.
There was every reason why he should be able to ally
himself with the ruler of some puissant country, and so
strengthen his duchy as well as his own position.

Whom should he choose? William looked about
him and set his mind upon Matilda, daughter of the
Count of Flanders. This was exactly the marriage
which his councillors would have chosen for him, not
so much because Matilda was beautiful, virtuous, and
skilled in the two great accomplishments of the day,
music and embroidery, but because the Count of Flanders was a man of great power. He had wealth and
soldiers, and, moreover, his family was of very high
rank. One of his ancestors had married a daughter of
King Alfred the Great, so that Alfred's blood ran in
the veins of Matilda. The proud count must have had
much respect for William's achievements, or he would
never have allowed his daughter to become betrothed
to the offspring of a peasant, the grandson of a tanner.

Now just at this time a number of princes were
forced to do penance or were even excommunicated,
for breaking the laws of the church concerning marriage. The haughty Count of Flanders must have been
very indignant when he was forbidden to give Matilda
to the duke, and there is surely no doubt that William's
wrath rose when he was forbidden to marry her if she
was offered to him. No one knows just why such a decree was passed. It may have been because of some
relationship between the two, or possibly because the
count was an exceedingly independent vassal and the
church did not wish him to increase his power by

forming an alliance with the strong Norman duchy. At any rate, the highest church authorities pronounced their decree that William and Matilda should not marry.

When William had once set his mind upon a thing, that thing usually came to pass. He was never impatient, he could wait, but he must have his own way in the end. He had determined to marry Matilda of Flanders. His council was with him, and neither the Count of Flanders nor Matilda seems to have made any objection. The church had forbidden the marriage, to be sure, but William did not give it up on that account. He kept up his friendship with the count, he sent legates to Rome to try to win the permission of the Pope, and then he waited.

But he did not take his seat on the ducal throne and fold his hands. There was much to be done. Many a proud noble still paid his homage to Arletta's son most unwillingly; but it was paid, and William was in peaceful control of his own country. The Count of Flanders was his friend, and the king of France was his ally—for the time, at any rate. William began to think of making a visit to England.

About fifteen years before he was born, his great-aunt, Emma, and her husband, the king of England, were driven from the English throne, and fled to Normandy with their two little boys, Edward and Alfred. Soon the king died, and in a very short time Emma married Canute, son of the man who had thrust her husband from his kingdom. She seems to have had no affection for her boys, for she left them in Normandy, and even agreed in the marriage contract that they should have no claim to the English throne.

These boys remained at the Norman court, and were treated very kindly by Duke Robert's father and then by himself. Robert even made an attempt to invade England in their behalf, and get possession of the English throne for them. Alfred was finally killed in trying to regain his father's crown; but Edward, after living quietly in Normandy for almost thirty-five years, was invited by the English people to come to be their king. He was nearly twenty-five years older than William, and had known and cared for the young duke in his boyhood. Since William was fourteen, they had never met. Naturally, Edward wished to see him. William always clung to his relatives with as warm affection as they would permit, and he was more than ready to cross the narrow channel that lay between him and England.

In these days, their wish to see each other would have been enough to explain the journey, but in the eleventh century it was a rare thing for two princes to exchange visits merely from friendship. There was generally a good reason for their staying at home, since in most countries a revolt would break out if the king was absent; and in this case, we are perhaps safe in thinking that Edward had a plan for his young cousin's advancement, and that William had at least a suspicion of what it was.

However that may be, William set out with a great train of nobles and attendants. They wore their finest array. Their ships were gilded and ornamented.

The figurehead of William's was an image of Rollo, the first duke of Normandy, and from the mast floated the pennant of the present duke. They carried to the king gifts of noble steeds, beautifully embroidered cloaks, handsome armor, and, it may be, some of the precious relics that Duke Robert had sent home when he was on his pilgrimage.

A warm welcome King Edward gave them. The lad of fourteen whom he had left in Normandy had become the man of twenty-four, tall, strong, manly, and with a reputation of wielding a sword that won its way wherever he unsheathed it. It was hardly a strange court to which he had come. Although Edward's father was a Saxon, his mother was of Norman birth, and from early childhood till near his fortieth year the king had lived in Normandy. He had always spoken French, and now he gathered Normans around him in his court. The highest offices in the kingdom he gave to Normans. These men had not forgotten their own country, nor the little son of Duke Robert who had become this masterful ruler of lordly Normandy. When they looked at him, they could well put aside the thought of the peasant mother, and remember only that he was a man whom they might be proud to have at the head of their homeland.

A merry time they had. There were feasts and tournaments and hunting parties, and there were long "progresses," or journeys through the kingdom, to show the Norman guests the cities and castles of the country. Edward was inclined to be meek and humble, and he always preferred to live simply and with as little of display as possible; but whatever William's virtues were, meekness was not the leading one among them, and he did enjoy having a touch of magnificence to whatever was going on around him. To please his guest, Edward made these "progresses" in a much more sumptuous style than he had ever favored before in travelling about his kingdom. The Normans who dwelt at the English court were delighted, but the Saxons looked at the swarms of foreign guests with some displeasure, and a little fear of what the result of the visit might be.

"What do you think of this sudden outburst of hospitality?" said one Saxon noble to another.

"I suppose a king must entertain his guests," said the other.

"True," said the first; "but we are Saxons in a Saxon land, and our king is half Norman by birth and wholly Norman by feeling. He has given the great bishoprics to Normans. Normans build their strongholds when and where they please. The officers of the king's household are Normans. We are under Norman rule. We call our country England; and we say that we are free, but—"

"But we are only a province of Normandy," said a third, who had stood by them listening grimly to their talk.

"We have the king of our own choice," said the second, "and he is a good, kind man. Don't you remember when they showed him the great casks of gold, the tax that the people groaned over so loudly,— don't you remember that he looked at it for a minute without a word, and then he said, 'This shall never be collected again; I can almost believe that I see little exulting demons of cruelty and extortion dancing on every barrel'? Was he not a good king to say that?"

"Yes, but he said it in French," said the third noble. "A king who does not speak the language of the country may be king of the land, but he is not king of the people."

"But he is almost a saint," said the second. "Only yesterday I heard some one call him the 'Confessor.' They say that he can work miracles, too, just like a real saint, and that if he touches any one who has scrofula, the disease is cured; and I have heard that more than once he has foretold what was coming to pass, and it came just as he said."

"It is of what may come to pass that I am afraid," said the first. "Who is to be king when this 'Confessor' dies? He has no children. There is no man in all England who can be called his rightful heir. He is Norman, his language and his feelings are Norman. What is more natural than that he should try to bequeath the throne to this Norman cousin of his?"

"And this is what the visit of Duke William and his roisterous crowd of knights signifies," said the third. "This is why all this elaborate entertainment which is never given to our own nobles when they go to court is lavished upon this Norman gang. We are fighters. Do you call out your men. I will call out mine. We will spread it through the kingdom. Never shall this foreigner, this son of a—"

"Gently, my friend," said the first; "what could we do? The king has the treasury and the arms and the castles and many soldiers. Shall we take a little band and march up to his gates and say, 'Come down from the throne, for I don't like to have you there'?"

"And so you would have us stand by in silence and fold our hands while our kingdom is taken from us?" demanded the third.

"What has been done? The king is receiving a friendly visit from a favorite cousin. May not a man receive a visitor and entertain him in the way that is most pleasing to the guest? They say that William has come here intending to pay homage to King Edward. Would you drive away a powerful vassal from our kingdom?"

"When one does homage, it is for some gain," said the third. "William of Normandy needs no aid from this side of the water to rule his duchy. All that he can want from England is—England itself."

"King Edward cannot give away his throne; that belongs to the country, not to him," said the first. "He is a Norman and looks at things in a Norman fashion, and he may promise to help William to get it; but that means more than a peaceful 'I give it to you' from Edward, and a grateful 'I thank you' from William. It means an attack by sea and land. It means that Saxon blood will flow to save the land, and that Norman blood will flow to win it. When that time comes, we will fight."

"But after all, Edward is a good man," said the second, "and they do say that even to bathe in the water in which he has washed his hands will often cure sickness."

From this discussion the second noble went away with more devotion to the king than ever. The third went home to count over his retainers, and to think upon how many brave men he could depend in case of a sudden uprising in behalf of William. The first, after a little time, sent a messenger secretly to a trusty friend in Normandy to suggest to the Count of Eu that this time of William's absence would be an excellent opportunity to raise a revolt.

"He may be killed in the fighting," thought the Saxon noble, "and at least, it will take him away from the court of England."

Meanwhile the festivities went on. Minstrels, jugglers, feasts, hunting—there seemed to be no end to the pleasures of the entertainment that King Edward gave so willingly to his cousin and guest.

CHAPTER IX

WHAT HE HAS HE HOLDS

"AND what do you think of my misty kingdom?" asked King Edward of the Norman duke.

"That it is misty, but that it is a kingdom," said the duke laughingly, "and it is a kingdom that may become very great."

"It may, but only under a great king," said Edward. "My brother Alfred should have been the king. If my mother—but no, we will not speak of her. Alfred would have ruled it well. He would not have been unworthy of him whose name he bore. I am better fitted for the cloister and the cowl. Have you thought seriously of the matter for which I wished you to come to England?"

"I have," said William.

"You see what the land is and what the people are," said the king. "These English are a blunt race; not stupid, but slow. They can do a thing and do it well if it once occurs to them that they can do it. They make far better jewelry than we, but it has not yet entered their heads that they can build as fine churches as we.

For their homes they are satisfied with what some of our villeins would despise; and it is all because it has not yet occurred to them that they can do better."

"It has occurred to them that they can eat and drink," said William.

"Yes," said the king; "and their feasts are not feasts, they are simply times of stuffing. They do not eat and drink to enjoy, but to see how much they can hold. One might as well shovel stones into a quicksand."

"They have a strange-sounding language," said William.

"Not a word of it do I know," said the king. "All around me are Normans. The Bishop of London is a Norman, and so is the Archbishop of Canterbury, so are all the people of my household. I must have men whose speech I can understand, and besides that, these English are fit only to serve Normans, not to rule them. But to our subject. You have done homage to me as to your liege lord, and I have promised you the crown of England at my death. Whether the English have any law about who shall follow me, I do not know, but surely a crown should belong to him who wears it. Be that as it may, I give it to you. I have not forgotten the kindness that your grandfather and your uncle showed me when I was a boy in Normandy, and I have not forgotten that your father lost ships and money in his attempt to give me the throne that belonged to me. I have much more to say to you, and tomorrow—"

"What is it?" asked the king, for a servant had drawn aside the curtain that hid the doorway. The servant bowed before the king and the duke.

"A messenger from over the seas would see the Duke of Normandy. He says that his errand is speedy and brooks no delay." Involuntarily William laid his hand on his sword. The king smiled at the motion.

"We will hope not," said he; "and yet to a soldier like you, to use the sword is to win glory." The messenger was admitted. He was travel-stained and dusty, and his dress bore every mark not only of a hasty journey but of a hasty departure from home. His Norman courtesy was almost forgotten, and after a slight obeisance to the king, he turned quickly to William and said:—

"My lord duke, there is trouble in Normandy. The Count of Eu rebels against your authority."

A hasty farewell did William and his knights bid to King Edward. Straight across the channel they sailed, and before the revolting count realized that they had left the shores of England, he found himself a prisoner in his own castle. Bold man as he was, he trembled and asked for conditions of surrender.

"Surrender without conditions," was William's reply, "or we storm the castle." The count remembered Alençon and surrendered. What should be done with the rebel was the next question. A hasty consultation was held between William and his barons.

"The count is a traitor. The punishment for treason is death," said one stern warrior, leaning on his shield.

"It is the custom of the country and a fitting penalty," said another.

"The Count of Eu is the cousin of my father," said William. "I will not send my own blood to the death of a traitor."

"He lived the life of a traitor," said a baron grimly, "and we are living the lives of honest vassals. We are giving you our blood and our service without stint, that there may be peace in your land. Will you hold back from just vengeance the man who is overthrowing all that we are trying to build up?" The young duke sat in silence a moment. Then he said:—

"My barons, you are older and more experienced and perhaps much wiser than I, and it might well be that I should yield to your advice on the battlefield and in the council-chamber, but this is neither. The Count of Eu is conquered. He has submitted. There is no more battle."

"There is council, though, or there ought to be," muttered one of the barons through his beard; but his ruler turned upon him fiercely and said:—

"There is not. By council a traitor may be hanged. So be it; but I am the duke, and I say that the cousin of my father shall *not* be hanged. Banished he may be, hanged he shall not be."

"The young eagle begins to feel his wings," whispered one soldier to another, and not without a secret delight that their ruler had again shown himself to be one that would rule.

"If the traitor is once in the hands of the duke," said the other, "and is allowed to live, every traitor in the duchy will rise up against us."

"Then he must never be in the hands of the duke," said the first; and so among them they contrived a way by which the count might quietly disappear from the place of battle and make his escape. Every Norman rebel knew where to go when he was exiled from his own country, and the count fled straightway to the King of France. Henry had forgotten all about the assistance that William had given him. He greeted the count with much honor, and soon received him as one of his vassals and gave him a goodly piece of territory.

This revolt was a small matter, but there was trouble of a more serious nature to follow. Duke Robert had left two young half-brothers, Malger and the Count of Arques. The count had never been friendly to William, but he had made no open revolt, and had even fought under the duke's banner. Malger was a priest, and William by the advice of his council had made him Archbishop of Rouen. No tie of gratitude bound Malger, and although he readily accepted the high position, he determined to use his power to overthrow the nephew who had given it to him, and to put the Count of Arques on the ducal throne. No son of Arletta, said the archbishop, should ever hold the place of his brother Robert.

Some years earlier William had intrusted to his uncle the county of Arques, and the count had at once built a strong castle. It was on a narrow tongue of land, while the keep, standing on a hill at the point near where the tongue joined the mainland, shut off all hostile approach. Around the keep the count had dug a fosse of unusual depth and width. William had reason to suspect his uncle's loyalty, and therefore he filled this castle with a garrison of his own men whom he thought he could trust. Unfortunately, either they feared the threats of the count, or else they were not able to resist his bribes. At any rate, they soon swore allegiance to the revolter.

Straightway there broke out all over the district of Arques a frenzy of theft, robbery, and murder. Men who so readily broke their oath of fealty could not be trusted to keep their hands from the property of others. They seized upon the goods of merchants, and the crops upon which the very lives of the peasant farmers depended. The church, too, was a constant sufferer. Church and peasant united in an appeal to William.

The duke was at Valognes when the messenger came. Without an instant's delay, he buckled on his sword to set out for Arques.

"The King of France is making ready to assist the Count of Arques," added the messenger. William stood with his hand on his horse ready to spring into the saddle.

"Say you so?" he asked sternly. "Is this the truth that you are telling me?" The messenger raised his right hand.

"Strike this off if you find me false," said he. William dropped his horse's rein, and stood for some minutes silent and in deep thought.

"Be it so," he said half aloud. Then he turned to his waiting knights.

"Let those who love me follow me," he said; and they set out on as wild a gallop as that on which William had once before set out from this same castle of Valognes. They spurred their steeds. One horse after another was exhausted. Twice William's horse sank under him, and twice he sprang upon a fresh one. When he came in sight of the castle of Arques, his faithful knights were far behind him. Only six could endure that frantic ride. Just what William expected to do with six men against a mighty castle no one knows, for happily some loyal vassals had called out three hundred knights. Even this force was slender enough, so the vassals told him, for the whole district was in rebellion.

"All the more need to quiet one part of it," said the duke. "When those rebels once see me face to face, they will yield." William's courage aroused a new hope in the others. Wild shouts of loyalty and enthusiasm echoed and reëchoed. The faithful nobles waved their swords, their shields, their lances, anything, as they rallied eagerly about their commander.

"There they are!" he cried. "Let every brave man follow me," and he galloped furiously toward the hill. His quick eye had seen a company of the rebels winding up the steep. They were evidently returning from some marauding expedition, for they seemed to be carrying great loads, and their horses went slowly and wearily. Without a glance to see whether any one was supporting him, William galloped on, and his brave men followed. The men of Arques were overtaken close to the castle gate. They fought for only a few minutes, then they retreated to the castle for their lives, and the great gates closed behind them.

"They shall yield," cried William, "and not a drop of loyal Norman blood shall be shed." More of the faithful knights had arrived. Between the keep and the mainland, William dug a deep ditch and built a palisade. Then he put up quickly a wooden tower to shut off food and allies.

Inside the castle were the rebels, the Count of Arques and all the vassals whose military service he could command, together with many more whom the aid of his archbishop brother had enabled him to hire. Outside the castle were William's men, and on the way to help the rebels and to crush the faithful Normans between the castle and the forces of the king, came Henry, ruler of France, and sworn protector and friend of William of Normandy.

William might possibly have conquered the rebels before him, but the army of the king, coming upon him in the midst of the battle, would almost certainly have given the victory to the men of Arques. The whole district was in an uproar. No one knew from what direction aid might come for the rebels. Leaving part of his army to defend the wooden tower and shut off any hostile troops that might appear from the east, the duke set out to intercept any that might come from the other directions.

It was not long before some loyal friends sent word to the brave besiegers in the wooden tower that King Henry and his men were encamped not far away, ready to come to the aid of the castle of Arques. None too many men had the besiegers, but a party started at once to prevent the coming of the allies, slipping away silently in the darkness that the rebels might not know that the numbers of their foes were less.

Morning came, and the French soldiers started out merrily. The young knights caracoled their horses. They sang old love-songs, and they laid wagers with one another about how high the sun would be when the men of this troublesome duke would flee before them like so many crickets. Then they formed in marching order. First came the soldiers armed with pikes and battle-axes, a formidable advance-guard. Behind them followed the long train of baggage, engines of war, loads of weapons, tents, and provisions for themselves and for the beleaguered garrison. With this were the "scullions, cooks, and carters," whose business it was not to fight, but to care for all these things. Then came the king and the whole troop of horse and foot, well armed and ready to engage in whatever conflict might arise.

Steadily the long line marched on. Victory lay before them; they had no thought of fear. It was a pleasant, sunny way. Little birds sang over their heads, flowers were under their feet. One stalwart soldier stooped to pick a tiny white blossom. The next moment he lay dead with the little white flower fresh and fair in his stiffening hand. An enemy's arrow had struck him; and there was the Norman band, only a little company, so little that the Frenchmen laughed and shouted exultantly and turned upon them.

The Normans fled. Whither? No matter, it was easy to follow and capture them; and with cries of derision the whole force of the king pursued. Into a narrow valley ran the Normans, with apparently no thought save of escape from their foes. On either side were steep, heavily wooded hills. The Normans ran, and the Frenchmen followed.

Suddenly a hissing storm of steel-tipped arrows burst upon the lines of the French. Not a foeman was in sight save the disordered ranks that were fleeing before them, but high up on the hills on either hand were William's good archers. Behind every rock and every tree they had stood so motionless that the shy little animals of the wood had forgotten their first alarm, and had begun to run fearlessly about their feet. The disordered troops of the Normans instantly faced about, formed in line, and fell upon the French forces. These, shut into the valley by the Normans, were thrust back upon their own troops. Everywhere there was disorder and confusion. In the clouds of dust and sand, friends and companions in arms struck wildly at one another. The horses, bold to meet danger face to face, were terrified by a peril that they could not see. They freed themselves from all control, and ran wildly wherever there was a moment's break in the flash of swords. Still swept over them the terrible storm of arrows from the unseen foe. Lance and gonfalon were

STILL SWEPT OVER THEM THE TERRIBLE
STORM OF ARROWS

trampled into the dust. There were great writhing masses of dead and wounded; and, through it all, past where the happy little white flowers had grown and the yellow sunshine had brightened the mossy ground around them, there began to trickle slow, sullen streams of the red blood of brave men.

Part of the army, led by the king himself, formed a wedge, and worked through to safety from immediate attack. They even went as far as Arques, but William's men were too strong for them, and they withdrew to the French boundaries, the king mortified and angry, and the soldiers talking sullenly to one another.

"Where is our vanguard, and where are our wings? What has this mighty king, this great man of battle, done with them?" And another would say:— "Has he any more mousetraps to lead us into, this wise and valiant ruler of ours?"

Duke William, having prevented any aid from coming to the castle from either hand, returned to the wooden tower, not to fight, but to wait. Why should one fight when hunger would do the work? The Count of Arques had contrived to send a messenger to Henry begging for help, but no help came. The castle was swarming with defenders, but there was no food. To have many men is good in a fight, but it is not good in a famine. The white flag was run up.

"Promise us safety of life and limb, and we yield," said the starving garrison. The gates were thrown open, and out came a miserable company. With faces worn and haggard, and drawn by the pangs of hunger, tottering along on feet that could hardly support them, and resting their hands on horses that were too feeble to bear the weight of their masters—to see the proudest knights of the land in such a plight was indeed pitiable. Nor was this all; for some of them, knowing well that death was the punishment for such treason as theirs, and fearing that William's promise would not restrain his just resentment, came out bowed down by the weight of the saddles that were strapped to their shoulders, hoping by their humility to disarm his anger.

To William's honor be it said that he inflicted no further suffering upon these miserable men. He did not banish the count. He even permitted him to retain nearly all of his estate; and when the count finally withdrew of his own accord to the court of Boulogne, William granted the land to another member of the same family.

William had paid a visit to England, and he had returned and conquered a revolt in his duchy, but there was another matter which he had not forgotten in all his feasting and fighting. Matilda of Flanders was to be his wife, and he had waited for the Pope's permission about as long as his impatience would permit. Some five years it had been since he was forbidden to marry her, and for five years he had waited with apparent meekness and obedience to the Pope's command.

He was in a different position now from that of five years earlier. He was at the head of Normandy much more perfectly than he had been before, for he had shown that what he had he could hold. Moreover, he had good reason to believe that in due time he would be king of England. Was a king and duke to be refused a dispensation that any ordinary knight might hope to obtain? The Normans had powerful settlements in Italy. Jealousy and war had arisen, and the Pope had been a captive in the hands of the victorious Normans. He had thought of the Normans as a wild, only half-civilized people, and expected from them the most severe treatment. Much to his surprise, the Norman commander came to him at once in person and addressed him most respectfully, inviting him to the Norman camp, not as prisoner, but as guest. All the chief officers attended the Pope to the camp. The greatest courtesy was shown him, and he was entertained for several days with as much luxury as a camp could furnish. Then with a guard of honor, he was conducted to the city where he wished to remain. Leo IX was a sincere man. Understanding the nature of the Normans better, he absolved them from censure, and even blessed their arms. These Norman warriors had opposed him sword in hand. Would he who had so readily pardoned them refuse a dispensation to the greatest Norman of them all? William thought not. To give permission in advance was one thing; to pardon what was already done was another.

So it was that Duke William took matters into his own control and appealed to the Count of Flanders for the hand of Matilda. The count was pleased with the powerful alliance and gave with his daughter a generous dowry, land and money and costly robes and priceless jewels. A ruling sovereign must be married in his own territory, so the count set off with his daughter and a long procession of knights and nobles to cross the district of Ponthieu to the Norman frontier. A brilliant company it was. The ladies were in elegant attire, their mantles sparkling with jewels and gleaming with many rich colors. The knights wore their armor, and it shone and flashed in the sunshine. The horses were richly caparisoned, with bright stones glowing here and there in their trappings.

At Eu, the first castle over the Norman frontier, William met his bride. He wore armor, and his helmet and mantle both flashed with precious stones. So magnificent was this mantle and that of his bride, that both garments, together with the duke's helmet, were presented to the cathedral at Bayeux and were kept for at least four hundred years. The whole company rode to the church of Eu; and there some priest, who trusted to the power of William to free him from the censure of the Pope, pronounced the blessing of the church upon the couple who were to become the ancestors of the English sovereigns of to-day.

There were celebrations and feasts and entertainments of all sorts; then with all the honor that Normandy could show, the maiden of Flanders was escorted to the Norman capital of Rouen. The Count and Countess of Flanders and all the Flemish court accompanied her, and at Rouen there were again many days of festivity and merrymaking.

The Flemings went back to their own land, and William with the greatest pride and delight took his bride on a royal progress to see the towns and people of Normandy. It had been thirty years since Normandy had had a duchess, and this beautiful, cultivated woman found a sincere welcome wherever she went. The church dignitaries might be pleased or displeased; the masses of the Norman people rejoiced.

CHAPTER X

A VOICE FROM THE CLIFF

T HIS marriage is thought to have taken place in 1053, when William was probably twenty-five years of age. His whole life had been a warfare, and one of his three decisive battles had been fought before he was twenty years old. This battle was Val-ès-dunes, and his victory settled the question of his supremacy in Normandy. He had conquered his own duchy, and he had shown that in all Europe there was no better commander than he. Two other great victories lay in the years before him. Nothing came to him by gift; everything must be won. Even for the hand of Matilda he had laid siege, and he had waited as he would have done to capture a city. His love for his wife was as earnest as was his vehemence on the field of battle. At last a gleam of happiness had come to him; but clouds were gathering, and in all his joy there were mutterings of a rising storm, of a battle that could not be fought with sword and lance.

"What do you think of our duke's marriage?" questioned a Norman knight of a priest.

"The lady Matilda is a gracious and beautiful woman," replied the priest.

"You priests are so cautious," laughed the knight. "Think you that the Pope will bless the marriage?"

"The gift of prophecy was not bestowed upon me," said the priest, smiling at the knight's apparent discomfiture.

"What would you do if you were Pope?" questioned the knight shrewdly.

"I am but a simple priest. Never could I even think of myself in so exalted a position as that of Father of the Church."

"I see there is no getting anything out of you," said the knight good-humoredly. "We'll drop it; but priest or no priest, I fancy that you know something about a good horse when you see one. Come with me on a hunt, and I'll lend you the best horse that you ever mounted. I presume you can think of some one who would be the better for a little wild meat."

The hunt was successful, and on the return the knight said:—

"To make a man a priest does not seem to make him a coward. That was a close thing when the boar attacked you. Ought a bishop to be braver than a priest, and the Pope braver than a bishop?"

"I don't know about that," said the priest; "but at any rate, the Pope is no coward. They say that he picked up a leper who was at his door, took him on his shoulder, and laid him in his own bed. A man who will do that is a brave man. He cares not a straw who opposes him. He means to work reforms in the church, and when he has once said what he believes is right, there is no power that will make him change." The priest made his farewell, and the knight looked after him with a grim smile.

"They all tell the same story," said he. "Sometimes it needs only a question, sometimes a cup of wine or a ride, and sometimes a horse; but they all think alike. The Pope will never bless this marriage. There's a chance for Malger, and there's a chance for King Henry—and, mayhap, there's a chance for me," and he spurred his horse and rode away in the direction of the Norman capital, where abode Malger, Archbishop of Rouen.

With the custom of giving high positions in the church to any young relatives for whom the head of a powerful family might wish to provide, there could hardly fail to be bishops and archbishops who were unfit for their office. No one doubts that Malger was one of these. At the head of the church in Normandy he was, the chroniclers declare that more than one pope had refused him the snowy pallium, the sacred vestment which was the sign of his ecclesiastical rank.

At this man's door the knight knocked. Sounds of feasting and high revelry came from within. After some delay the door was opened a little way, and the servant said, with a grimace that one might interpret as he would,—

"The archbishop sees no one to-day; it is a fast-day."

"I think he will see me," said the knight. "Come here." He whispered a single word. The door was flung open, and in five minutes the archbishop had excused himself from his guests, and he and the knight were talking earnestly together in a private room, far away from listening ears.

"The trouble is that no one can foretell what that turbulent nephew of mine will do," said Malger; "he can turn in as many ways as the fiend himself."

"True," said the knight, "but what can he do? He has a sword, and he knows how to wield it; but there are knots that even so keen a weapon as his will not cut."

"Nine-tenths of the nobles in the duchy favor the marriage," said Malger.

"Yes, so eager are they to have an heir to the throne and a hope of lasting peace that they will favor anything," said the knight; "but there need not be peace unless you will it. It all lies in your hands. Think of it! An excommunication—an uprising—help from a certain foreign power—the Count of Arques on the ducal throne—and would your brother dare to neglect the weapon by which he had won his place?"

"But would the Pope support an excommunication that I might pronounce?"

"You mean that he does not always manifest a hearty approbation of what seems to you a desirable course?" said the knight with a knowing smile.

"That is perhaps a gentle way of putting it," said the archbishop ruefully.

"And has it occurred to you that if he sees you so zealous in the discharge of the duties of your office, so eager to uphold his decree that you even venture to oppose the will of a ruler like the duke—do you not think that you will win the favor not only of the Pope, but of all the powers of the church? You have a high position, but even you may rise. There are other fields than Normandy." The knight gazed fixedly for a moment at the archbishop's face. Then with a careless obeisance he withdrew. As he went from the house, he whispered to himself exultantly:—

"I've done it. Now for King Henry and a rich marriage and a great feoff."

Straightway Malger issued a decree of excommunication against William and Matilda, the two children of the church who had so boldly ventured to disregard her authority.

Well might Archbishop Malger say that no one could foretell the deed of his nephew. Without delay William laid before the Pope proofs of Malger's unfitness for his office. The Pope could censure William's marriage, but he was none the less bound to consider impartially a complaint of this kind coming from the ruler of a great duchy. The proofs were only too plentiful, and two years after the marriage the archbishop was deposed.

A louder voice than Malger's now spoke. It was the voice of one Lanfranc, prior of the convent of Bec. Lanfranc was a scholar, with an eloquence and logic worthy of his descent from a famous family of lawyers, a man whose honesty and keenness of intellect had won for him the favor and the confidence of the Norman duke. This was the man who, with nothing to gain by his opposition and much to lose, now spoke out boldly against the marriage, blaming equally duke and duchess.

The same madness which always seemed to overcome William at any insult offered to his mother, now burst forth at this censure of his wife. He drove Lanfranc from his convent and banished him from Normandy. His wrath knew no bounds. He ordered part, at least, of the lands of the monastery to be ravaged and some of the buildings belonging to the abbey to be burned.

Lanfranc prepared to leave the Norman territories, but he took care to withdraw by a road where he was almost sure to fall in with the duke. The exiled monk wore the humblest garb that his convent could furnish, and he was mounted on a lame horse—some say a horse with but three legs. A single servant, whose dress was certainly no better than that of his master, followed the man who had been at the head of a great convent and the friend of a great duke. William met this little procession face to face. Lanfranc and the lame horse made a simultaneous bow. The combination was irresistible, and the duke's stern lips twitched with grim amusement at the sight. The prior saw his opportunity. Pretending great eagerness to hasten, he belabored his poor beast and said:—

"Pardon, pardon, my lord, that I am so slow to obey your command. Indeed, I am going as fast as I can, but if you would only give me a better horse,—if you would perhaps exchange with me,—I should be far more obedient." Whoever got the better of William in a jest had won the day, and he said:—

"Never before did a criminal ask a gift of his judge. Supposing that I should not only give you a horse, but should more than make up all that you have lost, what would you do for me?"

"Whatever an honorable man can do for his prince," replied the prior steadily. William looked him full in the eyes.

"You know the thing that I want," said he, "and you know that you can get it if any one can. Will you do it?" Lanfranc was no coward. He returned to the full the searching look of the duke.

"William, Duke of Normandy," said he, "my own liege lord, many a favor have you done me, but not for all that you have done and all that it is in your power to do would I say that your marriage is according to the laws of the church to which we have both promised obedience."

"Go, then," said William angrily, "and never let me see your face again in Normandy." The duke rode away furiously, and Lanfranc hobbled along in the opposite direction. An hour later a cloud of dust arose behind the banished prior. It came nearer. Some one was galloping so madly that Lanfranc guided his sorry steed to the side of the road. The rider drew up his horse so suddenly that the poor animal almost fell backward. It was the duke.

"Lanfranc!" he called.

"My liege lord," answered the prior.

"Did you ever hear of such a thing as the forgiveness of a sin?"

"Yes, surely," said Lanfranc.

"You say that my marriage is not according to the law of the church. Very well. Will you go to Rome and say, 'The Duke of Normandy has broken a law of the church; but for pardon, for the Pope's confirmation of his marriage, he will as a thank-offering do whatever deed of charity the Pope shall command.' Will you say this, and will you do your best to bring it about?"

"I will."

"Then what are you waiting for?" cried William. "Give him the best horse that you have," he said to his attendants, who were standing at a little distance. "And do you," said he to Lanfranc, "do you get you back to your convent and put on your richest robes. Horses and guards will be at your door, and do you be on your way to Rome before the sun begins to sink. On the very day that a messenger arrives to tell me that you have secured a dispensation, I will rebuild all that has been destroyed; and I will give the abbey of Bec three times the value of what it has lost. As for you, if you are true to me, and if you prove yourself the man that I think you are, you shall one day hold positions that have never entered into your dreams. Now go." William embraced him and gave him the formal kiss of reconciliation, and the prior went on his way.

That William had a sincere regard for the welfare of the church is proved by the character of the men to whom he gave her highest honors in his duchy,—Lanfranc, Anselm, and Maurilius, men worthy in mind and in heart of all that the duke could bestow. His marriage manifested less of opposition to the law of the church than of confidence in her willingness to pardon. About a year after the marriage, his son Robert was born; and in his love for the child and the mother, the negotiations with the Pope and with his successors would have seemed slow indeed, had not his thoughts been so fully taken up by other matters that pressed upon him.

The king of France, a fickle, vacillating ally, had once shown himself a generous friend; now he appeared in the character of a bitter enemy. France had never ceased to look with envy upon the fertile expanse of Normandy. The French kingdom, strong or weak, as contrast with its neighbors might show it, began to fear before the ever increasing power of the duchy. Ought a vassal, who at best could not be called over-submissive to his suzerain, to control the district that shut France from the sea, even the very river whereon her capital was situated? Ought these Normans, only five generations removed from the heathen who had forced an unfortunate king to part with his territories, to hold a duchy which by its size, power, and position was a constant menace to the kingdom to which it owed service? Let William keep the northwest; the east should again belong to France.

So said the French, and King Henry and his army set out to overpower this too prosperous duke.

The plan was for Henry to lead one division of the army into Normandy from the south, while his brother made an attack from the north upon the country about Rouen. To meet the advance from the north, William trusted some of his well-tried nobles; but to meet the advance from the south, King Henry and his great band of allies, William would trust no one but himself.

The Norman fighters assembled—and stood still. The French forces swept into Normandy from the north. They burned and they pillaged and they murdered. Churches or dwelling-houses, old men, young men, women, or children, it was all the same to them; and with a ferocity almost as savage as that of the Danes in their most savage days they ploughed their way, leaving want and suffering and death behind them. They encamped in the town of Mortemer. Every day there was burning and pillage of the country roundabout; every night there was feasting and drunkenness.

Just what was William about? There must be no battle, said this wise general of twenty-six years, until the whole Norman force could be brought together; and so all that the Normans attempted was to save what property they could, and to cut off small bodies of men who had strayed from the French troops.

At last the Normans were strong, and one dark night they marched silently to the town of Mortemer. It was just at the break of day. After a night of carousing, the Frenchmen were lost in a drunken slumber. Was it a bad dream? The houses were all ablaze. Where were their arms, their horses? What had happened?

Was it the troops of Normandy or was it hosts of demons that were upon them? Half-dressed, half-armed, mad with pain, they were cut down on the steps, even in their beds. They attempted to fight their way out of the burning town, but the head of every street was guarded. They resisted furiously. From early in the morning till the middle of the afternoon they fought, but it was in vain. They were cut down till the little town was red with their blood.

A man of high rank was chosen to be the bearer of news like this to William's camp across the Seine.

"A Norman knight is riding swiftly up the hill," reported the sentinel.

"Our men are in trouble. Arm and make ready to go to them," ordered William; but the rider waved his gonfalon joyfully.

"There is no longer an enemy in Mortemer," said he; "all whose ransoms would be worth having are in the prisons of Normandy, the rest are slain."

"It is God that has given us the victory," said William reverently; "to Him be the thanks." King Henry was encamped not far away.

"Surprise routed one army," said William; "it may be that fright will rout the other." In the middle of the night the king and his men were aroused by a weird, solemn chanting from the top of a cliff which overhung their camp.

"Arouse, ye soldiers of France! Too long have your eyes been closed in slumber. Onward to Mortemer, to bury your friends who lie dead in the streets, slain by the swords of the Normans."

Before sunrise King Henry and his men had fled, caring for no plunder, no captives,—nothing but to get far away from the terrible duke.

The king was ready to make peace, and for three years there was peace. This was about as long as Henry could resist the temptation to attack the ever increasing power of the Normans. He set out with a great company of Frenchmen and their allies to plunder Normandy. With wrathful patience William gathered his knights together, and then again he waited. In Falaise he remained, while the Frenchmen cut a swath of fire and pillage through the country. Everywhere were William's spies, and when the moment came he struck.

Henry was on his return. He and his vanguard had crossed the river Dive at Varaville, and had climbed the cliffs on the eastern aide of the stream. The rear-guard and the great quantities of treasure that they had taken from the country had not yet come across. They were on a narrow causeway that was built out into the river at a place where it might be forded when the tide was low. William had secretly marched around the French lines, and now he fell suddenly upon the half of the army on the causeway. There was a terrible struggle, hopeless from the first. It is said that not one of the rear-guard escaped.

From the cliffs only just across the stream King Henry saw every movement. He saw his men struck down and taken captive, and to see was all that he could do. If his counsellors had not held him back, he would have plunged down the cliff in a hopeless attempt to rescue his knights; but the tide was coming in swiftly; only the most expert swimmers could cross the stream, and what could even they do with Norman arrows flying about them, and the lance and the terrible battle-axe waiting to receive them on the opposite shore? There was nothing for Henry to do but to save what men remained to him by a speedy flight from Norman territory.

This battle at the ford of Varaville was the end of the French invasions. Henry gladly made peace, and for the sake of it he offered to rebuild Tillières and restore it to Normandy. Two years later Henry died, and profiting perhaps by William's experience, he too threw himself upon the generosity of a foe, and left the guardianship of his little son to William's father-in-law, the Count of Flanders.

William had gained possession of his own country, and he had repelled the invasions of the ruler of another. He himself was to become an invader, but with a kind of lawfulness of claim so like that which is put forward a few years later that his conquest of Maine seems like a rehearsal of his conquest of England.

Count Herbert, driven from his inheritance of Maine, a large and fertile district south of Normandy, fled to William, became his vassal, and bequeathed to him the county of Maine.

"The land is mine, and I shall take it," said William; "but I shed no unnecessary drop of blood." With his usual policy of patience, he kept his hands from the chief city, Le Mans, but took one fortress after another and ravaged district after district. The people of Maine were finally exhausted. William held the whole country, and when he called upon Le Mans to surrender, it not only yielded, but flung open the gates with a welcome to William and to peace which was sincere in part, at any rate, for now there would be no more fighting. William had taken the city without shedding a drop of blood. Men greeted the duke as a saviour rather than a conqueror. Throughout the town his praises were shouted. A long procession swept out of the church chanting psalms of joy. He might almost have been entering his own Falaise, so great was the rejoicing.

William had yet another cause for happiness. Lanfranc had been doing his best in Rome, and finally the promised messenger came to William with the word that he had awaited so eagerly for six long years.

"The duke will not yield," Lanfranc had said, "and an interdict punishes the innocent in the kingdom as much as it does the guilty. Moreover, if the marriage is not confirmed, if by any means William should be forced to send Matilda back to Flanders, that will cause war. Ought not the Father of the Church to prevent bloodshed by mercy? Are there not heathen enough to kill without shedding Christian blood?"

Pope Nicholas yielded, and the marriage was formally confirmed by the church. The penance imposed was that William and Matilda should build four hospitals, one in each of the four chief towns of Normandy, and that they should build a convent for women and one for men. They obeyed, and the two noble abbeys of Caen are the memorial of the broken law of the church, of the penance, and of the pardon.

CHAPTER XI

PROMISE OR PRISON?

O CCUPIED as William was by revolts in his own duchy, invasions of the king of France, and negotiations to obtain the Pope's sanction of his marriage, he had never forgotten the promise of King Edward that some day he should wear the crown of England. He waited patiently, increasing his power in Normandy, and watching keenly every movement of the people across the Channel. Twelve years had passed before anything happened that seemed to strengthen his hold upon the English crown.

Now when "all folk chose Edward to king," the principal reason for their choice was that Edward belonged to the old Saxon family that had been their rulers before the coming of the Danes. One of Edward's chief supporters was a powerful noble named Godwin, Earl of Wessex, and he gave to the new king his daughter Edith in marriage. Godwin may have been indignant that Edward's gratitude was not powerful enough to make him obedient to the man who had helped him to the throne; or he may have been genuinely disappointed when he found that he had only exchanged Danish rule for Norman; for in education and taste Edward was as much of a Norman as if he had never left Norman soil, and to Normans he gave all places of honor in court and church. Whatever may have been the reason, he opposed Edward determinedly. The king accused him of the murder of Alfred, and the council seized his estates and banished him.

Soon after William made his visit to England, Godwin returned. He had cleared himself of the charge of murder, and the council gave back his land. It did more, for a decree was passed declaring that the king's Norman friends must leave England because it was their advice that had brought about such injustice.

An event like this could hardly fail to make it clear to the king that the English people would not give up easily to any foreign rule. Edward began to find that his recommendation to the council would not be enough to place William peaceably upon the throne. Would it not rather bring about discord and war? and would not the Danish party seize upon any time of disunion to force a Danish king upon the land? Was there anything better to do?

Far away in Hungary was a prince called the "Outlaw," a nephew of Edward's. He was invited to England, and now the question seemed to be settled, for his father had been greatly loved by the English people; but in a few weeks he died. His son was too young to be thought of as ruler of the land, and again Edward must try to plan for the succession. He had learned that the king could not give away his crown; but he had also learned that when the people came to make their choice, the wish of the king would be of great weight. What should he do?

Godwin was dead, but he had left a son, Harold, and every day Harold's power was on the increase. He had no claim to the throne by blood, he was merely the brother-in-law of the king; but William's relationship was only that of grand-nephew to Edward's Norman mother. No drop of English blood royal was in his veins any more than in Harold's. Edward's choice lay between a child of the royal family, whose youth would lay the kingdom open to Danish dominion; a foreigner of a race hated by the English; and an Englishman loved and admired by the English nation. Who could blame him if his mind turned toward Harold?

It came about one bright day in 1064 that Earl Harold went out sailing with a merry party. There were three vessels full of his friends. They started from Bosham, near the Isle of Wight. Just where they would go, they had not decided, but they took with them their dogs and hawks and bows and spears, for they meant to hunt wherever they landed. A storm came up suddenly. The boats were separated, and the one that carried Harold was driven across the Channel and wrecked. In the darkness he and several of the party were cast upon an unknown coast. Harold was the first to reach the land, and in the roar of the surf he shouted:—

"Ho, there, ho! Is any one saved?" There was no sound from the shore, but from the waves came a cry of "Help, help!" Into the fearful tumult of the waters Harold plunged in the direction of the voice. He touched a man in the darkness and brought him to land.

"The earl himself," said the man. "Glad am I that you are saved."

"And I, too," said another. "And I," "And, I" cried other voices. "It would have fared ill with us in England if we had gone back without the man who is to be its king."

"Talk not of kings," said the earl; "talk rather of where we are and how we are to escape. If we are on the coast of Normandy, I'd rather go back into the sea."

"The duke owes England nothing but kindness," said one of the party.

"He would willingly owe her for more kindness," said the earl grimly. "We will stay under these rocks till daybreak. They seem to rise up high above us; at least, it is darker there than to the right or the left; and when morning comes, we will try to escape. I would give half of my earldom to have a good piece of English ground under my feet once more."

Just before the break of day two men stood on the little cliff that in the darkness had seemed to tower so far above the beach. By their dress they should have been fishermen, but on the shore there were no signs of nets having been spread, and the men had neither fishhooks nor lines. Instead they bore stout ropes and long poles with strong hooks at the end.

"Stop!" said one softly, as the little path came near the edge of the cliff; "there are sometimes better things than driftwood, or kegs of food or bits of iron. Stay back and let me look."

"Yes, I know what you want. Stay back yourself," whispered the other angrily, and he flung his companion back heavily away from the cliff. The noise of the waves covered that of the scuffle, and the man crept to the edge and peered over.

Down below him was the little group. The sailor's dress and the knight's dress he could make out, but there was one man the richness of whose garments even the salt water could not entirely conceal. The watcher on the cliff noticed that some attempt seemed to have been made to lessen his discomfort. The cloak of one and the tunic of another were thrown over him. He moved, and the fisherman caught a glimpse of his face and started.

"I haven't been on the English coast for nothing," he said to himself. He sprang up softly, but the other caught him by the leg.

"Where are you going?" he demanded in a fierce whisper.

"To the count."

"Then I go with you," and he pursued closely as the first ran across the field. They were soon out of hearing of the shipwrecked party.

"What are *you* going to the count for?" called over his shoulder the one who had seen the group on the shore.

"Because you expect a reward from him, and I mean to have some of it," said the other boldly.

"You do? and what can you say to win a reward? I have something to tell."

"Tell me what it is, or you will never get to the count."

"And what would you have to tell, then? Would the count be pleased that you had killed a man who was useful to him? Watch and see that no one escapes, and I will give you a pound when I come back."

"You expect to get twenty, or else you wouldn't," muttered the fisherman; but there was nothing else to do, so he gave up the pursuit. The spy ran on, but before he came to the castle he met the count.

"Count Guy," said he, "I have a bigger fish than I ever caught before. Will you give me twenty pounds for him? I'll warrant you he'll pay you one hundred. It's the Earl of Wessex."

Without a moment's delay, the count summoned his followers and rode to the coast. The broken vessel had come ashore, and the shipwrecked men were trying to make it seaworthy. So busy were they that the first they knew of the coming of the count was his call,—

"Hold, you are my captives!"

"Who are you?" demanded Harold defiantly.

"Count Guy of Ponthieu, a faithful vassal of Normandy. You are my prisoner."

"I claim of you the hospitality that one noble has the right to claim of another," said Harold.

"You do not give me your name," said the count with a peculiar smile. "I know it, however. You are Earl Harold of England, and down into my strongest dungeon you go until your ransom is paid."

"And this is your Norman courtesy? You are thieves and robbers all, and so was your Rollo before you," said Harold fiercely.

"What the wave brings to us is our own, be it weed or drift," said the count calmly.

"Or men?" asked Harold angrily.

"Or men," repeated the count. "The man who is wrecked is accursed of God, or God would have brought him safely to his haven."

"What kind of God you have in Normandy, I know not," said Harold bitterly; "but the God of England tells us to help the unfortunate."

"And so may you do when you are in England," said the count; "but this is Ponthieu, and I am lord of Ponthieu, and a faithful vassal to Duke William and—"

"And when did your faithfulness begin?" asked Harold scornfully.

"Long enough ago for me to have a castle. It has a dungeon and a torture chamber, too, and sometimes these will hasten the coming of a ransom."

Harold was taken to the castle, perhaps to the dungeon; but one of his faithful attendants who had been out of sight when the count appeared, remained in hiding until he and his captives were gone, and then made his way to Rouen and demanded to see Duke William. To him he told the story of the wreck and the capture, and begged that he as overlord would force the count to set Harold free.

It was a terrible temptation to set before the man whose ambition it was to become king of England. Here was his only rival fallen by the fate of the waves and the winds into the hands of a man whose anger the earl had already aroused by his boldness. He need do nothing but to let the count work his will. The dungeon and the rack might hasten the ransom, or they might hasten the death of the only man that stood between the Duke of Normandy and the succession to the English crown. He had only to imprison this messenger, and it would never be known that any appeal had been made to him.

Whatever William did afterward to further his ambition, his course now seemed most honorable. Swift messengers were sent to Count Guy to ask for the freedom of the English earl, to demand it if need be. Guy yielded gracefully, and accompanied Harold, not as jailer but as host, to the castle of Eu on the boundary line of Ponthieu. There Duke William received him with the greatest courtesy. Count Guy was rewarded with money and land, and Harold, Earl of Wessex, became the guest of William, Duke of Normandy. The two men who were most prominent in western Europe were together; what would come of the meeting?

Apparently the chief result of it was only a most hospitable entertainment. Harold was provided with the best that the castle afforded. There were feasts and games and hunting and hawking; and finally, there came the noblest sport of it all, so Harold and his friends thought, for one of the Breton nobles had revolted, and William invited his guests to join him in an expedition to overcome the rebel. They were successful, and when they returned, William gave them generous presents and knighted those who had not already received knighthood. It was a merry time.

"You have shown us great courtesy," said Harold to William. "Save for you, I might still have been a prisoner in the dungeon of the Count of Ponthieu. The silver I can return to you, but the kindness and the hospitality I can return only if you will become my guest in Wessex. May I hope that this will come to pass?"

"I thank you," said William heartily, and he added slowly: "Yes, I will come; but, Earl Harold, there is something on my mind that I wish to discuss with you. We have lived in friendly companionship, and it would not displease me if the relationship between us was even closer. You are a man of great power, and some day you will marry, and in such wise as to increase your power. How would an alliance with Normandy please you? I have a daughter Adelaide, nine years old, or eight—I will ask her mother. When my father left me to rule the barons of Normandy, he said of me, 'He is little, but he will grow.' So say I of my Adelaide. But here comes the little maid herself. Will you have her, Earl Harold? She's the fairest little girl in Normandy." He caught the child in his arms and seated her high up on his shoulder.

"How is it with you, Adelaide? Will you marry this Englishman and go across the water with him to live in the far-away land?"

"Will he take me in a boat?" asked the child earnestly.

"Yes, will you marry me?" said Harold.

"I've wanted to go in a boat ever since I was a little girl," said Adelaide. "I'll marry you right away; but wait till I call my dog, he wants to go in a boat, too. Come, father, you and mother, and we will go across the water."

So it was that the little daughter of William was betrothed to Earl Harold. A formal ceremony followed, and the child was much disappointed to find that she would not cross the water at present, but would only be led up to the altar in the church by this tall Englishman with a brilliant company of knights and nobles and ladies looking on.

Harold was older than William; the marriage was far in the future; and even if it came to pass, an alliance with the Duke of Normandy would be a great advantage, so the earl willingly agreed to the betrothal.

Harold had been entertained as a guest to whom the duke wished to show special honor; but for all that, he would, as he said, have given half his earldom to have a good piece of English ground under his feet. Several times he had named an hour to set sail for England, but when the hour had come, the duke had always had some excuse for detaining him. A wonderfully large wild boar had been seen in the forest, and his guest must join in just one more hunt; or the wind was not in the right direction; or the sky gave signs of a change of weather. These excuses were often so trivial that Harold well understood that, guest as he was, he was not at liberty to leave the Norman shores till it should please the duke to allow his departure.

The crown of England lay between these two men. Each knew that the other intended to win it, and Harold was not entirely surprised when William said:—

"There is another subject that I wish to discuss with you. Of course a man in the king's counsel as you are knows that it was settled some twelve or thirteen years ago that at my cousin's death I was to become king of England."

"The king does not reveal all his plans," said Harold evasively.

"True," said the duke quietly; "but I fancied that he had revealed this one to an earl who was so fully in his confidence. Edward is feeble, his life cannot last many years, perhaps not many months. We must be prepared for what may happen. Until that comes to pass which will come, I must remain in Normandy; but I need a strong man to look after my interests in England. I need not say that when the time comes, I shall look after his interests. He who serves me well now will have wide stretches of land and the highest honors of the kingdom. Will you promise me to act in my behalf and to do all in your power to secure for me the throne of England?"

"I will do all that I can to carry out King Edward's will," said Harold evasively.

"That may be enough, and it may not. Edward is advancing in years, and as one grows weak in body, he is sometimes influenced by those around him to make plans that he would not have thought of in his stronger days. Will you promise me—"

"Father," said a childish voice, "won't you come and tell the armorer to make me a sword? He won't, and I'm ten years old, and you had one when you were not nearly so old. You told me you did. Come quick, father." Robert seized his father's hand, and the great duke followed meekly to give the order to the armorer. When he returned, he seemed to have forgotten all about the English crown, and he said to Harold:—

"I think you have never seen the whole of the castle. Will you go over it now?" Up the narrow, winding stairs they went to the very summit of the tower; then down, down below the hall with its light and color and cheer to the wine cellars, and below those to the dungeons. Great pits they were into which no ray of light could penetrate. There was a noisome smell of slime and foulness.

"Count Guy spent two years in one of my dungeons; but I fancy that less than two years in this would make a man agree to anything," said William with a significance which Harold understood.

When they were in the hall again, the duke said quietly:—

"I may depend upon you, may I not, to act in my interest to the full, and to do your best to secure for me peaceable possession of the English crown? Do you promise?" The duke spoke gently; but his eyes were fixed upon Harold, and in them was a stern glitter like the flashing of a sword.

Harold was a man of truth, but he held many honors, and even greater ones were before him. At the last breath of Edward the English people were ready to make him king. Should he give up a kingdom and submit to a living death in the horrible dungeons of Normandy for a scruple of conscience? What was a word after all? Only a breath. Ought it to hold one like a chain of iron? Moreover, he must think of others besides himself. If he was down in that fearful pit, William would attempt to become king of England. There would be war. Ruin and devastation and bloodshed would sweep over the country. Had a man the right to keep his conscience pure at the cost of the whole land? These were not new thoughts to Harold, but in a moment they flashed through his mind like a flash of lightning. He yielded.

"I will do it," he said, "I will do my best to place you peaceably on the throne of England."

"And all that the man who sits on the throne can do for another, will I do for you," said William; "and the day after to-morrow, if you insist upon going, all our merry company will ride to the shore with you and see you safely launched on the blue waters of the Channel.

Morning came, and with it a message from the duke.

"My knights are assembled in the council hall. They are come to do you honor before you depart from our court. Will you come with me to receive their farewells and their good wishes?"

Harold rode with the duke to the great council chamber. There was a brilliant assemblage of knights and nobles and ladies of the court. They seemed to have clustered about some object in the centre of the hall, but as William and Harold drew near they separated. There stood the richly carven chair of state. Over it was thrown a cloth of gold, and on this were the holy vessels brought from the nearest cathedral. In the centre was a missal open at one of the Gospels, and near it lay some of the relics of Saint Candre.

"I know well that you are a man of your word," said William to Harold, "and your promise is enough for me; but for the sake of those about me, to increase their loyalty and their confidence, I ask you to swear on the Gospel and on these relics that you will do everything in your power to aid me to become king of England."

To the people of the eleventh century an oath was far more binding than an ordinary promise, but Harold had gone too far to go back, he thought; and although William spoke in a most friendly way, his eyes were sternly bent upon the English earl. Harold hesitated for a moment. The thought flashed through his mind, "Saint Candre is not a very powerful patron. I need not fear him. I will do penance, and I will make great gifts to the church, and I will win over every other saint in the calendar to be my friend." So Harold laid his hand on the Gospels, as William bade him, and took the oath. Two priests, who had stood one on either side of the chair of state, gently lifted the golden cloth. There was silence through the great hall; and Harold turned white with horror, for under the golden cloth were relics of the most powerful saints of Normandy, and relics that Duke Robert had sent from Rome and from Jerusalem. Upon these relics he had laid his hand as he took the oath, and if the oath was broken every one of those saints was bound to be his enemy and to do him harm. No wonder that he was aghast.

"A promise is a promise," said William in his ear. "To a man like you, whose promise is sincere, it matters not that he has sworn to it on the holiest relics that the church in Normandy possesses." He turned to his knights:—

"Our good friend and welcome guest has told me that he must set sail for England in the morning. Let us give him a merry escort to Harfleur, and see him fairly embarked on the water that perhaps will not always separate the interests of Normandy from those of England."

Never had William's knights seen him so full of jests and gayety as on their return from Harfleur. They did not know that he was saying to himself over and over:—

"If he keeps his oath, it is well; if he breaks it, who is there in all England that will trust the kingdom to a man who is forsworn?"

CHAPTER XII

ON BOARD THE "MORA"

T WO years later, on January 5, 1066, King Edward died. That same day saw the meeting of the council to name his successor. The choice was soon made, but not without free discussion.

"I give my word for the crowning of Edgar," said one gray-haired councillor.

"Edgar is but a child," said many voices.

"He is of the royal blood," said the old man. "Never has England of her own free will bestowed her crown upon one who was not of the house of Cerdic."

"Shall a few drops of blood in the veins of a child count for more than the valor in the heart of the man who has been the real sovereign of England for more than ten years?" said another councillor. "There is no one else in the land—or out of it," he added, with a withering glance at a little group of men who were suspected of being Norman in their sympathies—"there is no one else whom the people of England love and admire and trust as they do Earl Harold of Wessex, and I give my voice for him as the successor of our holy King Edward."

"And yet it is said in Normandy that many years ago the holy king gave his word that the Duke of Normandy should be his successor," said the boldest of the little group in the farther corner.

"Have the Normans who have come to our land been so true and upright that we should trust even an unproven rumor of their country?" retorted a knight fiercely.

"No king can bequeath his crown," said another councillor gravely; "that is the gift of the people; and, moreover, this is, as you say, but a rumor, while we know by the testimony of many witnesses that the king in the last hour of his life recommended Harold as his successor."

"Holy men at the hour of death have often new vision and strange powers of prophecy," said the abbot of a great convent. "It is not well to pass lightly by what men see who see more than men can see." The vote was taken, and Harold was elected with hardly a dissenting voice. Two great chieftains bore to him the slender golden crown from the chamber of the dead king.

For a moment Harold hesitated. His wise use of his abilities had raised him to the highest position in the land; it was a time to be proud. But was it all his wisdom, was it not the course of events? Would not another man with his opportunities have done even more? it was a time to be humble. And in the doorway stood the two nobles with the golden circle which he had solemnly promised to give to another man. It was a forced oath—no, it was not, his word was his own;

he had chosen, a hard choice, but he had chosen. He would refuse and say boldly, "Come what may, I will not live a man forsworn. I cannot be your king." What freedom that would be! But the councillors were speaking:—

"We bring the crown of England from the chamber of King Edward. We are come to say that it is the will of the council that you, Harold, Earl of Wessex, should be our king. Do you accept the crown?"

"The will of the council." That was the way of escape. He had no more right to refuse the crown than a king had to give it away. He was but a tool, a weapon of the people. Should the sword say, "Why choose me? I will not be chosen." So said Harold to himself. Again he yielded, and as he had once said, "I will promise," so he now said, "I will be your king."

The times were too full of danger for a land to remain for a single day without a lawful sovereign. Before the next nightfall, Westminster Abbey had seen the burial of Edward and the coronation of Harold.

William of Normandy was hunting in the forest near Rouen. He had bent the bow which no other man had strength to bend, and he had taken aim at a deer, when from behind him came a voice, "My lord!" The arrow flew wide, and the deer sprang away.

"How dare you?" said William, turning upon the man fiercely. "I have forgiven rebellious vassals, but I never yet forgave a man who spoiled a shot like that."

"Pardon, my lord," said the man who had spoken. "I have a message for you from one over the water. Edward has ended his life, and Earl Harold is raised to the kingdom." William turned deadly pale. His bow fell to the ground. He laced and unlaced his mantle. Then without a word he strode to the bank of the Seine and motioned to his boatman to row him across. He went up the hill to his castle and entered the great hall. He looked to one side, then to the other. He dropped upon a bench, and with his mantle thrown over his face sat leaning against a pillar. The men in the hall withdrew silently into little groups.

On the hunt with William had been one William Fitz-Osbern, son of the faithful guardian whose death had once saved the life of the duke. He alone ventured to speak to his master.

"Duke William," said he, "this is no secret. Every street in Rouen is ablaze with the news. This is no time to mourn that Edward is dead or that Harold is forsworn. This is the time to cross the water and seize the kingdom that is your own."

William straightway sent an embassy to Harold, demanding the keeping of his oath. Harold replied that it was better to break a bad oath than to keep it; and that in any case the crown was not for him to give, but for the nation. It was plain that to win the kingdom William must fight for it. He appealed to his vassals.

"Many years ago," he said, "the English crown was promised to me by King Edward, and this was right, for I am his lawful heir. When Edward had become a feeble old man, Harold usurped his power and turned the English people as he would. Harold belongs to an accursed race, for to his father is laid the savage murder of Alfred. In your very presence he swore on the relics of the saints that he would uphold my right—not my right, but that of Normandy, for Alfred was supported by Norman arms, and the relics were those of the greatest saints of our land. He and his father together drove the Normans from England. Shall we not avenge the wrongs of our own countrymen?"

Lanfranc, who had won the Pope's confirmation of William's marriage, was ready to place his keen intellect at the service of the duke, and now an appeal was made to Rome. To the Pope the matter was put as a missionary undertaking. William was going to England, it seemed, to punish a usurper and a man forsworn, a man who had not only stolen a kingdom, but who had insulted the saints, whose good deeds were the most cherished possession of the church. Would the Father of the Church judge between them? The Pope decided in favor of William, and sent him a consecrated banner and a ring containing a sacred relic.

While the embassy was in Rome, William called together his vassals at Lillebonne and asked their aid. He could not command it, for a vassal was not bound to cross the sea with his lord. They were not enthusiastic.

"England is rich," said one, "and Harold can engage even kings and dukes to fight for him."

"Yes," said another, "we cannot win; and if we attempt it, we shall only ruin our own Normandy."

"I would gladly follow you over land and sea," said one, "but I am poor; I cannot furnish ships or even arm my men as they should be armed for such an attempt."

"Harold will grow stronger every day," said a noble. "Whatever is done should be done at once; but England has a great fleet and well-trained sailors. More than one year, more than two years, would it take us to prepare ships to meet it." Then came forward bold William Fitz-Osbern.

"You have fought for the duke," said he, "but has he done nothing for you? You owe him service for your feoffs; and what matters it whether you fight on one side of the water or the other? The ground is the same. Shame on the faithless vassal whose chief must beg for his obedience. There is something more," he added. "You know the temper of the duke. Is he one to yield? Has he ever yielded? If you refuse him now, what do you think the end will be? He is angry. He has left your assembly. Shall I beg him to return?"

Even the boldest of the barons were alarmed. They did, indeed, know William's temper. "Speak to him for us," they said to Fitz-Osbern.

Fitz-Osbern spoke, but in accordance with his own wishes, and without the least regard to those of the barons.

"Your barons have such zeal in your service and such affection for you," he said, "that they will gladly meet all danger into which you may lead them." The barons looked at Fitz-Osbern angrily and motioned him to stop, but William sat by with stern, lowering face, and they were silent. Fitz-Osbern went on:—

"To punish the wicked usurper, the scorner of Norman arms, the insulter of Norman saints, I will furnish sixty ships, well filled with fighting men; and every man here will agree to furnish not the number of men to which he is bound, but twice that number."

Then the wrath of the barons broke out. There was no attempt to keep order. The hall was full of angry, shouting men, each struggling to be heard. Now was William's time. He was no longer the stern ruler, but the fascinating pleader; and when William chose to persuade rather than to demand, few could resist him. One by one they yielded.

This expedition was setting out to avenge a broken oath and an insult to religion. The Pope had blessed the enterprise. The ships would sail under the banner of the church. This was more profitable than a pilgrimage. A man might gain the good-will of the powerful ruler of Normandy, who would perhaps be king of England; he might have a reasonable hope of winning land and gold; and he might be working for the good of his soul, all at the same time. So advantageous a bargain as that was seldom offered. No wonder that soldiers came from near and from far. No wonder that all the seaport towns were building ships, and that all the inland towns were forging armor. Night and day the anvils rang and the hammers beat.

As has been said before, there was always danger in a sovereign's leaving his country, if only for a short time. As far as possible, William must secure the friendliness of the surrounding districts. As a vassal of France, he went to Philip, son of Henry, to offer him a share in the conquest of England. Philip and his councillors had already discussed this project of William's, and they were prepared to oppose it. "Normandy," said they, "is so independent as it is that her vassalage is only a name. Let her win England, and it will not be even that." So when William came to Philip and said:—

"I come to you as my suzerain to ask if you will assist me to gain my rights in England and to punish a usurper. If you will help me, I promise to hold England, as I do Normandy, as a feoff of the kingdom of France." Then the young Philip replied rather pertly, inasmuch as he was speaking to a man much older than himself and the greatest military commander in Europe:—

"And who will care for your duchy while you are trying to gain these rights of yours across the sea?" William looked down upon the young fellow before him and answered:—

"That is a matter which need not trouble my neighbors, for God has given me a prudent wife and loving subjects, and together they will care for my duchy."

William then invited his wife's brother-in-law to join with him, but young Baldwin asked first what he would gain by it. William never could pass by the opportunity for a jest, and even in this hurried time he stopped to fold a blank parchment into the shape of a royal missive, sealed it with the ducal seal, and on the outside he wrote:—

"Brother-in-law, in England you'll win
Just as much as you find within."

Afterward, however, he made generous promises to Matilda's relatives for their aid.

The last thing before setting out to join his
forces, William solemnly appointed Matilda ruler of
Normandy during his absence; and that in case of his
death his son Robert, a boy of twelve or thirteen,
might be already in power, he put him in nominal
command of the military forces of the duchy. There
was a great assemblage of the chief men of Normandy
when Matilda was formally declared "Duchess Regent," and at the end of the ceremony William said
earnestly:—

"We beg that you and the ladies of your court
will give us your prayers that the blessing of God may
go with us and may give us success."

At the mouth of the Dive, not so very far from
the ford of Varaville, whence King Henry and his men
had begun their wild flight from the land of the
Normans, assembled the ships, seven hundred, one
chronicler puts it; three thousand and more, others say.
Ships came and men came, grave and dignified barons
and wild, turbulent young adventurers; no easy horde
to keep in order, but the duke was able to control the
power that he had aroused. Plunder was forbidden,
and the rule against it was enforced. The cattle and the
cornfield of the peasant were untouched.

So strict was the order maintained that a man who had hoped to make his way through the camp by his Norman dress and his knowledge of the Norman tongue, was captured at once and brought before the duke. He was an English spy, but William received him like a guest, treated him courteously, and finally sent him away with a message to Harold. "Tell your lord," said he, "to go where he thinks himself safest, and if he does not meet me there before the year ends, then need he never fear me while he lives."

Harold had some reason to be comforted by the message, for day after day passed, and still the fleet was weather-bound at the mouth of the Dive. September came. The north wind blew and the rain fell and the surf pounded on the shore. No ship could go to sea in safety, and for one long month the whole fleet waited impatiently for the south wind that should speed the vessels on their way to England.

Not only did the south wind fail, but provisions began to be scarce. It was easier to move the fleet than to bring food; and so, at the first breath of the west wind, William took the ships to Ponthieu, and anchored off the mouth of the river Somme. Still the south wind refused to blow. The soldiers murmured.

"Where are the fertile lands that this great conqueror promised?" said one.

"Here is land enough," said another, "I want to get out on the water;" and one who had been gazing out over the sea turned and said:—

"The terrible comet that swept through the sky, we thought that it meant ruin to England, but it is borne in upon my mind that the two long fiery trains that trailed after it portend rather that Normandy shall be divided and shattered by this evil plan of Duke William's to seize upon land that God's ocean has separated from us."

"He is mad," said one. "His father had the same madness; and when he, too, set out to conquer England, the winds opposed him, just as they oppose Duke William. God is against him. Let us leave him and go to our homes."

The little church of Saint Valéry was not far away, and William alternately offered prayers at its altar and watched the vane on its spire. Finally he arranged a solemn procession of the clergy of the church bearing the relics of their patron saint. Gold and silver and jewels were cast upon the shrine until it was almost buried beneath the offerings. Duke and army prayed, and at last, after six weeks of waiting, the wind blew from the south. The ships made ready to set sail for England.

But a great warship was coming into the harbor. No one had ever seen it before. It was all a-glitter with its bright decorations, and its sails were of many colors.

"I have no vassal," said William, "who could bring me a ship like that. It must be from some other country."

"But there are the three lions of Normandy on her sails," cried Fitz-Osbern. As she came nearer, William saw that the figure-head was a child, a boy wrought all of gold, and in his hand was an ivory horn. As William looked at it he fancied that it was like his little son William; and so it was, and in the boat was the Duchess Matilda with her attendants. The name of the ship was the "Mora," the "Delay," and she was a gift from Matilda to her husband.

"As you have been delayed by foul winds," said the duchess, "so now shall the 'Delay' fill her sails with fair winds and bear you swiftly to the land that is of right your own."

"So shall it be," said William, "for the 'Mora' and no other vessel shall carry me across the water." The consecrated banner was run up to the masthead. Matilda said her farewell, and to the music of cymbals and pipes and many other instruments William set out for England.

Harold's months on the English throne had not been easy. The Norwegians, aided by his own brother, Tostig, had descended upon the north coast, and he had been obliged to march beyond the Humber to repulse them. So it was that when William landed at Pevensey, not a blow was struck, though if the south wind had blown but a few days sooner, an army would have been ready to receive him. William was the first to spring ashore, but in his eagerness he fell at full length. A low groan of fear came from the soldiers.

"It is a terrible omen," said one.

"God is against us," said another; but William rose with a bit of turf in either hand and said jubilantly,—

"So it is that I take seizin of my rightful kingdom." A soldier pulled a handful of thatch from the roof of a cottage.

"Here, too, is seizin," he said, "of England and all that is within it."

"I accept it," said the duke, "and may God be with us."

After one day the whole force marched to Hastings, where provisions could more easily be procured. A wooden fortress was put up and a moat was dug. William did not wish to go far inland, so he set to work to harass the country round-about that he might provoke Harold to come to him. By forced marches Harold came southward, and when he reached London, William's messenger met him.

"This is the word of the Duke of Normandy," said the messenger: "By Edward's will and by your own oath I call upon you to give up the kingdom."

"And this is the reply of the King of England," said Harold: "So long as a man lives, he has a right to alter his will, and in no court is an extorted oath held sacred. I offer you my friendship and costly gifts if you will depart from the land without violence or harm; but if you persist in grasping for that which is not your own, then will I and my brave men meet you in battle on Saturday, and as we have just driven an invader from our northern coasts, so will we drive you from our southern."

Few days were there before the one that was set for the battle, but Harold took a little time to go to his own church at Waltham. Many gifts he laid upon the altar, then he knelt in prayer for the forgiveness of his sins and for the welfare of his land. "I sought to do for the best," he prayed, "but it may be that I am entangled in the meshes of evil. Forgive me, and save my country from the usurper, and give the victory as shall be for her own best good."

Harold went back to London and there met him his faithful brother Gyrth, who pleaded with him:—

"Do you stay and defend London. A forced oath is not binding, but yet it is an oath, and I fear that God will be against you. No oath have I sworn. Let me go forth to meet the invader. If I am slain, then can you, the king, gather another army and avenge me; and let us now burn the houses and lay waste the harvest fields and leave this invader with nothing but the desert and the sea. So will he go to his ships and betake him to his own country." Then spoke Harold:—

"No friend of mine," said he, "shall go forth to face danger that I ought to face. Never will I set fire to an English home or lay waste an English harvest field."

And so it was that Harold of England went forth to meet William of Normandy.

CHAPTER XIII

"ENGLAND IS MINE"

THE strength of the Norman army was its horsemen; the strength of the English army was its
foot soldiers. While William's forces were well fitted to
make an attack, Harold's power lay in his ability to resist an attack. William was a great commander, for he
knew when to advance; but Harold was hardly less
great, for he knew when to stand still. He was familiar
with southern England, and on his hurried march from
the north he had mentally chosen his position. It was
seven miles from Hastings and on the direct line from
Hastings to London.

Just below the summit of the hill of Senlac he
arranged his men in order, those on either hand armed
with clubs or javelins or forks or even stone hammers
or sharp stakes. In the centre, where the first advance
of the Normans was expected, were the veterans of the
army, soldiers tried and true. Their shields and arms
were much like those of the Normans, save for one
terrible weapon, the great battle-axe. This had a longer
handle than the Norman axe, and in the hands of a
strong man it was the most deadly of weapons. In the
midst of the veterans was the dragon banner of Eng-

land, and the king's gonfalon bearing a warrior in full array. Near the banner stood Harold and his two faithful brothers, Gyrth and Leofwine. Stretching along in front of the line of soldiers was a strong palisade.

This was the array which the Normans were advancing to attack. At the first sight of the English encampment they paused to put on their armor. William's coat of mail was brought out, and by mistake the front and back were reversed. The soldiers who were to bear their part so boldly in the battle trembled before the omen of evil, but again the quick-witted duke smiled at their fear and said:—

"I trust in God, not in signs and warnings; but if this is an omen of anything, it means that just as I change this hauberk about, so am I to be changed— changed from a duke into a king."

William, too, had arranged his men in three divisions, the Normans in the centre. In the first line were the slingers and archers; then came the heavy-armed infantry; and behind them rode the knights in full armor with the lance and the sword. In the centre of the group the holy banner of the Pope waved in the breeze of the early morning, and under it were Robert of Mortain, a brave, faithful, kind-hearted man; and Odo, Bishop of Bayeux, who, forbidden by the church to bear sword or spear, solved the difficulty by arming himself with a war-club. These were the sons of Arletta and Heriwin of Conteville. Between them rode their half-brother, the great duke. No lance or javelin did he carry, but a heavy iron mace, as terrible a weapon as the axe of Harold.

On toward the hill came the Norman array, but suddenly a man rode forth in front of the line. It was Taillefer, the minstrel. He sang songs of Roland and of Charlemagne; he made his horse curvet and caracole; he tossed his sword into the air and caught it as it fell. He chanted words of encouragement to the Normans and of threatening to the English. Both armies stood as if spellbound. The minstrel waved his sword to the duke.

"Duke William," he said, "long ago, in happy Falaise, you promised me one day that whatever gift I should ask of you, you would grant. This is the gift— to strike the first blow against the usurper." Then, wheeling about, he dashed up to the English line, thrust his lance through one man, cut down another with his sword, and in a moment lay dead, struck down by many an English weapon.

The Norman line advanced. Straight up the hill they charged. "God help us!" they shouted; while the English veterans cried, "Holy Cross! Holy Cross!" Harold had laid his plans well. The palisade, the wall of shields, the solid ranks of men—as long as these were unbroken the Norman onslaughts were as powerless as a shower beating upon an oak tree. Duke William and his men fell back. The ranks were in disorder. The whole invading force was panic-stricken.

"Flee, my duke, save yourself!" shouted a soldier.

"The duke is dead! The duke is dead!" cried some one, and the wild cry ran through the lines. William uncovered his face and pursued his men.

"Come back," he called; "why do you flee? I live, and by the grace of God I will conquer. Come back, or with my own hand I will strike you down."

At the head of the Normans William dashed forward for another attack. His horse fell under him. No matter, he could press nearer on foot. He struck down Gyrth, and his brother struck down Leofwine; and now the English fought for vengeance. William mounted another horse. It was slain. He mounted a third. The Norman forces pressed on. The wooden palisade was beginning to yield, but behind it were the deep ranks of brave Englishmen, and their firmly grasped shields were a stronger wall than any palisade.

Something more than daring was needed. Part of the invading force advanced, turned, broke ranks and fled. The raw troops of the English rushed from their position and pursued, though the veterans at their left shouted "Back! back!" for this was the old trick which the Danes had played upon the English two centuries before, and which William had played upon the king of France. The Normans wheeled about, formed their lines anew, and cut down their scattered pursuers.

It was almost twilight. Since nine in the morning the battle had raged. To attack the English behind the firm line of shields was like making an assault upon a fortress. William ordered his archers to shoot straight up into the air. There fell upon the English a storm of the deadly steel, the most terrible event of the day. Men held their shields high up to protect their heads.

Then was the moment for the Norman lance and the Norman sword.

Harold fell, his eye pierced by an arrow. His own veterans fought to the death; not one was captured, but the less disciplined troops fled madly over the hills to the northward. They knew the country, but their pursuers were lost in the morass or fell headlong over the precipice; the land itself was avenging the death of her heroes. The English turned and took a fearful revenge on the invaders; but this was only a little company—the battle was lost. If those Englishmen who left their lines to pursue the pretended retreat of the enemy had been as true to Harold in deed as they were in heart, if they had been as obedient as they were courageous, then might the battle of Senlac have been an English victory instead of an English defeat.

The body of Harold was probably buried by William's orders on the shore near Hastings, and sometime later removed to the dead king's church in Waltham; but there is a legend that many years after the battle there was seen in far-away Chester a monk blind in one eye, bent and bowed with trouble and sorrow, and that on his death-bed he owned that it was he who had once been called Harold and crowned king of England.

After the battle the Normans returned to Hastings.

"What is the duke going to do?" said one soldier. "Will he not march upon London?"

"They say not," said another. "They say that he declares God has decided between him and Harold, and that he will remain in Hastings to receive the homage of the nobles of the land."

"Will they come, do you think?"

"Neither William nor I can tell that."

"And what you two can't tell, no one knows," said the other with a laugh.

The English knew that William might march directly upon London. A new king must be chosen at once, and the council met without delay. A strong leader might have united England and saved her; but there was none. Worse than that, there were several parties. One favored the child Edgar, son of the Outlaw; one said that the victory at Senlac was the judgment of God, and that to refuse to submit to William would be to resist God; and the northern earls stood aside, willing that the kingdom should be divided if only they might have a share. Finally Edgar was chosen as king; but he was a child, and the army had vanished.

William waited five days in Hastings for the homage which did not come; then he set out on a march to the eastward as far as Dover, and from there directly to London. Wherever the English yielded, he was mild and gentle, and repaid generously any damage caused by his soldiers; but wherever there was the least resistance, he was so severe that many a town surrendered without a blow. The chief men of England met in London.

"The Duke of Normandy is ravaging the country roundabout," said one. "Soon we shall have nothing around us but burned dwellings and fields laid waste. He is merciful where men yield, and brutal where they resist. I counsel that we yield."

"Harold gave his life to repel the invader," said another, "and shall we so lightly resign the liberty for which he died?"

"We do not resign it, it is already taken from us," said one; "the only question is whether we shall lose our lives as well as our liberty."

"But is our liberty gone?" said another. "Canute came as a conqueror; but he ruled like an Englishman. Has not this duke made Normandy the power which she was not before his reign began?"

"True," said a thoughtful man who sat near him. "Canute came of a heathen race, but he was a good king. This William is a faithful son of the church and—"

He may be a son of the church, but he is the grandson of a tanner," said one bitterly. "Such a disgrace has never before fallen upon the throne of England."

"We cannot resist him," said one sadly; "we have no choice."

"What should we do if we had a choice?" asked another, looking hopelessly about the room. "We chose Harold; he is dead, and there is no one to follow him. We chose Edgar, but he is a child. It may be that it would have been wise, even of our own free will, to choose this great commander, and hope that he would do for us what he has already done for Normandy."

So it was that the crown was offered to William. He had fought for it fiercely, and he had put aside indignantly the suggestion that he should make a compromise for gold and treasure; but now that it was offered, he hesitated. He would have no weak point by which any one else might demand it of him as he had demanded it of Harold. He called a council of his chief officers.

"England is mine," he said. "God has chosen between me and the usurper. In time to come, I shall rule every sod and every stream; but now my word is obeyed and my voice is feared over but a small part of the land. Shall I take the crown before I have won it?"

"Then would a king ever have a crown?" asked a keen-eyed councillor. "Is a king ever sure of his kingdom? Can he ever say that no insurrection will arise, no revolt that, however small, shall yet make him the less king until it be subdued?"

"True," said the duke thoughtfully; "perhaps you are right, though when I am once come to my kingdom, I think there will be no revolts to fear. There is another reason why I should wish to delay the crowning. Do you remember that over the sea is your duchess, my own dearly beloved wife? It is she who has freed me from the care of my duchy that I might cross the water and claim that which is my right. Whatever I win of honors and glory belongs to her, and I would gladly have her beside me to share my crown."

"If you are crowned at once," said another councillor, "it will be taking what is your own as soon as it is possible; but if you delay till you have conquered England step by step, then will you seem not like the rightful king kept out of his own for a time, but like an invader who seizes the land, field by field, and when he has grasped it all, then says that he is king."

Arrangements were made for the coronation. It had long been the custom for the Archbishop of Canterbury to place the crown upon the head of the newly chosen king; but there was some doubt whether Stigand of Canterbury had been made an archbishop with all the due formalities, and as William meant that no one should ever question his legal right to the throne, he chose the Bishop of York to lay upon his head the new crown all ablaze with jewels which had been made for this occasion.

English and Normans filled Westminster Abbey, waiting eagerly for the glittering procession. The clergy in their richest vestments, the English lords in their splendid mantles gorgeous in coloring and sparkling with gems, the royal guard in their brightly burnished armor, swept up toward the altar. There was a moment's break in the long line, and people held their breath to watch, for towering above the spectators, handsome, grave, and stately, came the great duke himself. On one side of him walked Stigand; on the other, Ealdred, Bishop of York.

The Te Deum had been sung; there was silence. Then Ealdred of York and the Bishop of Coutances, who had come with William from Normandy, took their stand, one on either side of the altar. William came forward and stood before the multitude. Then spoke Ealdred of York:—

"This man who now stands before you is William, Duke of Normandy. I present him to you with the blessing of the church upon him. Is it your will, O you people of England, that the crown of England shall be laid upon his head?" Then spoke the Bishop of Coutances:—

"And you, O you Normans, is it your will that he who is your duke shall rule a twofold empire? that he who governs the duchy of Normandy shall become the sovereign of the people of England?"

"Yes! yes! King William! King William!" shouted the whole assembly. But William, who had so many times faced death on the field of battle, turned pale and trembled. There were wild shouts of "Fire! fire!" outside the church. Was it the Norman guards who heard the cries of assent within and mistook the clamor for an attack upon the duke, or was it one last effort of the English people to rid themselves of this foreign ruler? No one knows, but the buildings around the church had been fired, and the blaze shone through the many-colored windows and cast a strange, weird light upon those who were within.

The solemn ritual went on. There was prayer and litany and chanting of psalms. There was swinging of censers, till rich clouds of incense rose far above the altar. William kissed the cross which had been carried before him when he entered the church. Then he laid his hand upon the Gospels; and it may be that there came to him a thought of the oath which he had driven Harold to take, and that he trembled at the memory of this rather than at the fire and the tumult.

"Do you solemnly swear," said the bishop, "that you will rule your people according to the laws of the land?

"Do you swear that you will do justice and mercy to all that abide within your realm?

"Do you swear to be true to the church, to watch over her interests, to guard and defend her?"

William, still trembling, made the sacred promise. Then was he anointed with the consecrated oil, the glittering crown was laid upon his head, and the Duke of Normandy was also King of England.

The coronation should have been followed by the ceremony of paying homage, but this had been prevented by the fire. William was as wise as he was bold, and he thought it best to withdraw to Barking; and there it was that one Saxon noble after another came to become "his man." William received them as his own beloved subjects, invited them to hunt and to hawk, and treated them like favored guests. As a rule, the nobles dwelling in that part of England which had submitted paid William a fee and received their lands again as a fresh grant from him. The northern earls seem to have been convinced that resistance would be useless, and they, too, did homage. William showed them special courtesy, and even promised one of them his little daughter in marriage. Nevertheless, he did not trust them to return to their distant north, where they might easily arouse rebellion, but he gave them each some high office that would keep them in his sight.

To the child Edgar, and his mother and his sisters, William did not fail to show honor; and for the boy himself, who came so near to being king, he seemed to feel a sincere affection. The whole policy of William was to shed no blood, to arouse no unnecessary ill-will, to be just and even generous to those who yielded to him; but to be mercilessly severe in his treatment of those who opposed him.

But there was a crowd of nobles from Normandy and the neighboring countries, and they would not fail to say:—

"King William, when we helped you to gain possession of your kingdom, you said, 'The land that I win, it shall be yours.' Give us our land as you promised us then," and William gave.

According to the ideas of the times, all land belonged to the king and was loaned by him to vassals on condition of their fealty. Now William was the king, crowned and anointed; therefore all who had opposed him were rebels and their land belonged to him. Godwin's family held large tracts, and these he might lawfully appropriate. Besides this, there were many estates whose owners and owners' sons had died at Senlac, and these estates would return to the sovereign. William did not try to make the English poor and the Normans rich; but he took from those who opposed him and gave to those who were loyal to him.

The king must have a well-fortified place of residence in London, and so it was that he began to build the Tower of London. At the same time, he gave the city a special charter. "Ye shall be worthy to enjoy all the laws ye were worth in King Edward's days," said William, and he kept his word. Nevertheless, the strong fortress arose, and it was well garrisoned with men from Normandy and the districts lying around it.

But the king of England was also Duke of Normandy, and across the Channel were lands which ought not to be longer without their lord. William had landed in October and been crowned at Christmas. More than two months had passed since then. He began to feel that he might spend Easter in Normandy with his beloved wife and children.

Nothing could seem wiser than his plan for the government of the kingdom during his absence. Those left in control were his half-brother Odo, the warlike Bishop of Bayeux, he who kept the letter of the church law by wearing no sword, but followed the desires of his own spirit by mounting a war-horse and galloping to battle armed with a war-club; and the second, William Fitz-Osbern, the old and tried friend who had first urged him to make his attack upon England, and who had tricked the Norman nobles not only into aiding him, but into aiding him to such an extent as they would never have dreamed of doing.

Odo and Fitz-Osbern were strong men, but trouble might arise. Since William would not be in the kingdom to suppress any revolt, he very wisely carried those who might become leaders of a revolt with him to Normandy—not as captives, by any means, but as an escort of honor. Each one of the most dangerous of the great men among the English had received a message somewhat like this:—

"William, king of England, is about to cross the sea. He would be escorted by men of mark in the kingdom over which he rules, and therefore he sends you courteous invitation to visit with him his duchy of Normandy."

Probably every one who received this message knew that he was to be taken to Normandy as a hostage for the good behavior of the men who were left behind. If William had demanded their attendance, they might have refused, though the refusal would have been a signal for a revolt; but he had invited, and invited with such flattering courtesy, such apparent confidence in their loyalty, that to refuse would be not only ungracious, but a most unwise confession of hostility. They accepted the invitation; and the ship "Mora," that six months before had brought William and his army to the shores of England, now set out for a return, bearing not only a king of England, but a company of English nobles who to do him honor had left their own land and were coming to Normandy.

Nor was English homage the only treasure on board the ships. Beautiful vessels of gold and of silver, adorned with precious stones, finer jewelry, more exquisite work of enamel and filigree of gold than the Normans could make in their own land, hanging lamps of iron and of the precious metals, the finest cloth of woollen and of linen, robes and vestments rich with embroidery, tapestries shining with gold thread, curtains made precious by the work of the needle—with such things as these the ships were loaded when he who had left his native land a duke returned to it a king. No wonder that he received a welcome. Here was the man who by his own hand had won glory for himself, had honored his duchy, had enriched his nobles, and had, as the weapon of the church, punished one whom the church deemed deserving of punishment.

CHAPTER XIV

"WILL YOU YIELD?"

IT was Lent when William landed in Normandy, but it became a season of rejoicing, for the whole land was wild with delight at the success of the duke. The Normans declared that he had brought over from England three times as much gold as there was in the whole of Gaul. Never had they seen such robes of state and such vestments for the church. They were especially curious to see the English nobles with their blue eyes, light flowing hair, long mustaches, and names that no Frenchman could pronounce. Most interesting of them all was the young Edgar. William did not recognize his claim to the throne, but he looked upon the boy as ranking highest among the English nobles, and treated him with special respect as well as affection.

The great celebration of Easter was to be held at Fécamp, the pretty town nestling by the little stream that flowed between the two ranges of hills. Here the great mass of the treasures and curiosities was brought, and here assembled William and his family, the English nobles, the Norman knights and higher clergy, and

William's many guests from among his allies who had helped him to win these treasures.

At Fécamp was the old church built by William's great-grandfather, Richard the Fearless, and here was the Easter rejoicing to be. Silken tapestries worked by English hands hung from the roof-beams. Flowers were placed in every little recess. In at the eastern windows the morning sunlight shone through the stained glass and cast slowly moving flecks of brilliant color upon the white and gold vestments of the clergy.

All was light and brilliancy. The gleam of the precious stones that adorned the holy vessels of the altar was reflected in the vivid coloring of the dresses of the ladies of the court. One wore a long green garment edged with a band of gold embroidery. Over this was a tunic of deep blue with a gold belt fastened with a red cord and tassel, while a red mantle, with lining of white silk, served as the "dominical," or covering which women must wear when receiving the Holy Communion. Another wore a tunic of soft cream-colored woollen with a red belt. Her blue mantle was clasped at the neck with a golden clasp set with garnets. In her hand she carried a small blue bag. Over her head and falling down her back was a long white veil. Beside her was the wife of a noble in a pink tunic edged with purple and gold. Her mantle was of purple lined with light blue, and about her neck was a double string of softly gleaming pearls. Women usually wore their hair either flowing loosely or in four long braids falling in front, two on either side of the face. Often their foreheads were all ablaze with bands of jewels. The men were hardly less gorgeous, for their mantles were of every color that could be dreamed of, and they were fastened at the shoulder by clasps set with jewels from which the light flashed at every movement.

Most of William's life had been spent on the battle-field, in besieging the retreat of an enemy, or in the gloom of some dull gray castle, and it is no wonder that the hour of safety and quiet in the midst of joyful faces and brilliant gala attire gave him a happiness which it was not often his lot to enjoy.

After the Easter service came the feast, and that was splendid with the spoils of England. The English guests winced when they saw the drinking cups made of the horns of the wild bull, and bound top and bottom with bands of gold, and the golden dishes, incrusted with glowing jewels of red and blue and green and yellow, which had been familiar to them in other scenes of feasting, brought forth to grace this celebration of their conqueror. They must bear and be silent; the time might come—who could tell?

Two months later the church which Matilda had built at Caen was to be dedicated, and this was another splendid ceremonial. Before the voyage to England, William and Matilda had vowed to devote their little daughter Cecily to a convent life, and on this day the child was brought to the altar, solemnly set apart from her brothers and sisters, and specially given up to the service of the church.

The whole summer was a time of triumph and jubilee for duke and duchess. From one end of the duchy to the other they travelled, receiving everywhere the highest honor that the people could pay, and leaving all behind them rejoicing in the generosity of the gifts that William bestowed upon nobles and clergy, such gifts "as neither king nor emperor had ever made before," say the old chroniclers with delight. To the knights he gave horses richly caparisoned, each bearing a helmet and a shining coat of mail. There were beautiful mantles and jewelled swords, and hangings for their cold stone walls. Well might England tremble, for there seemed no end to his treasures. To the churches of Normandy he gave ingots of gold; copies of the Gospels, beautifully written on vellum, whose covers were inlaid with gold and precious stones; relics of saints and martyrs in cases that were worth a knight's ransom; censers of glowing copper of most elaborate workmanship, made in close imitation of the temple at Jerusalem or the great church at Rome. To the Pope were sent still greater gifts, and among them was the captured banner of Harold, representing to the Pope his own increasing power and the fealty of him who was the most powerful sovereign of western Europe.

William had wished to remain in Normandy and spend Christmas with his family, but there was trouble in England. Although he was called king of the whole country, his actual rule was over only the southeastern portion. To leave a land, nominally his kingdom, but practically unsubmissive, in charge of two men who, however firm rulers they might be, despised the people who were in their care, and who permitted the Normans to rob and oppress them as they would, could hardly fail to bring about revolt, and revolt there was from one end of the land to the other.

Fortunately for William, this rebellion had no general leader, and the revolters were not united. The feeling of bitterness was universal, but it showed itself first in one place and then in another, so that William could deal with the uprisings one by one. Matilda was already addressed as Queen, and he had hoped to carry her with him to England that she might be crowned; but this was no time for any coronation ceremonies, so once more he left her in Normandy as regent. His son Robert was thirteen, and William directed that she should rule in the name of the boy. Then he set sail for his kingdom.

He did not meet the English as a conqueror who had returned hastily from another land to suppress an uprising, but as their king who was ready to show kindness to his loyal subjects. He held the usual Christmas court, and received with much courtesy all who came to it. He listened to their suggestions, and as far as possible gave them whatever they asked.

The centre of the revolt in the west was the city of Exeter, and Exeter had shut itself up behind its strong old walls with their towers and battlements, and had made no acknowledgment of the Norman invader as its lawful king. It was a rich, haughty old city, with citizens who were proud of their independence, and were determined not to yield to this "no man's son" from over the seas.

These citizens went at the business of a revolt with some idea of system and union. There were many foreign merchants dwelling in Exeter, and these they induced to join the struggle. To the neighboring districts they sent messages urging them to unite against the invader. In Exeter dwelt the mother of Harold, and her mourning for her three sons was a constant reminder of the destruction and death that had come with the coming of William.

To this proud old city William sent a message:—

"William, King of England, asks that his city of Exeter receive him within its walls, and that its citizens swear to be faithful to him." Then the citizens replied boldly:—

"We will pay the tribute that we have been used to pay, but we will not take any oath to the king, nor will we admit him within our walls."

"No subjects do I receive on such conditions," answered William, and rode straight toward Exeter, ravaging the land about the city.

"The king is encamped for the night but four miles away," reported a spy. Then there was much debate within the town about what should be done.

"Our walls are thick and strong," said one; "let him come."

"The king is a terrible man," said another; "it is of no use to resist him. Never yet did he fail to work his will in whatever way he would."

"It may be," said one of the older men, "that he does not understand that our city has always been independent. Let us send a company forth to meet him and parley with him; then can we tell better what there is for us to do." So a company of the older men went forth to meet the king and parley with him; but when they saw the array of soldiers, they hesitated; and when in the midst of the soldiers, with a strong guard on either hand, they saw the hostages, young men of their city, who had been sent to dwell with Harold as a proof of the good-will of the town, they stopped short.

"That is my own son," said one of the men in horror, "the one in the blue tunic and the red mantle. Who knows what this cruel king will do to our children?"

"He is angry," said another; "parleying will do no good." They went forward, but at the first sight of William's face they saw that parley would, indeed, be useless. For a moment they were silent. Then the father of the hostage came forward trembling and said:—

"King William, we beg your forgiveness for the wild speeches that have been made. We are sent by the citizens of Exeter to meet you. The town will yield and open her gates when you come near."

"Is this the speech of all?" asked William sternly.

"Of all," they answered.

"Then I will go forward, and if the city shall fling wide its gates and, man by man, shall swear fealty to me, then will I grant it a free pardon."

The little group went back half in hope and half in fear.

"What did he say?" called the citizens, crowding eagerly about them; but when they knew, then were they indignant.

"You were not sent to surrender, but to parley," they said angrily.

"But he has our hostages, and one of them is my own boy," said the old man huskily.

"Your boy is no more to us than another," said the citizens brutally. "You have betrayed us. He is only the son of a traitor. Let what will come to a traitor's son." Then they piled up arrows and great stones and strengthened their walls and their gates. So it was that when William came near, the gates were closed, and on the top of the wall were men who shouted speeches of defiance to their king. William's face grew white with anger.

"Bring forward a hostage," he ordered, and the young man in the red mantle was led forward in the sight of the citizens.

"Put out his eyes," said the king. The soldiers hesitated. "Obey," said the king. "It may be that the city will yield. Let one die to save many."

An old man on the wall was listening intensely. "Take me," he cried, "King William, take me, and let my boy go." The agonized voice reached even to the ears of the king, but he shook his head. The old man's clasp on the battlement relaxed, and he fell dead at the foot of the wall.

"Will you yield?" called the king, but the citizens answered by a volley of arrows.

"Fire!" said William, and a fearful return was made. The citizens shot again, and were jubilant as they saw one soldier after another fall.

"Bring boiling water and stones and spears and battle-axes," the citizens shouted, for little companies of soldiers were creeping up to the wall. They held shields over their heads, and the shields were needed, for arrows were fired straight down at them, heavy stones were rolled from the walls, and boiling water was poured upon them; but the arrows glanced off from the stout shields, the heavy stones rolled harmless to the ground, and even the boiling water did little injury. These men were dragging ladders, and slowly and carefully they put them up against the wall. Then, still under the shelter of the shields, the soldiers swarmed up boldly; but the citizens thrust at them with their spears, and swung their terrible battle-axes. Not a man could get a footing on the walls.

While all this hand-to-hand fighting was going on, William's men had brought up the unwieldy machines for slinging stones, and the arbalests, great crossbows on wheels, that would fire arrows with violence enough to send them through several persons. But the citizens, too, had slings and arbalests, and after seventeen days of such warfare William seemed no nearer victory than at first.

Meanwhile, afar off from the fighting, some of the soldiers had been digging a deep hole in the ground. Then they dug a tunnel from this hole toward the city, supporting the earth above them by strong wooden props. When they were sure that they were

HEAVY STONES WERE ROLLED
FROM THE WALLS

well under the wall, all the men left but one, and he soon followed them, setting fire to each prop as he went. Then the soldiers were drawn up nearer the city.

"See," cried the citizens on the wall, "he has stopped fighting. He will yield. William the conqueror is conquered. Let us—" But the wall was trembling under their feet. It shuddered and fell. The king's soldiers dashed through the breach, and the city was taken.

"What shall we do?" wailed the citizens. "He shows no mercy. Remember Alençon."

"In the name of the church we will go to him and beg for mercy," said a priest; and out of the open gates there went forth a pitiable company. First came the clergy bearing the cross, the Gospels, and the sacred vessels and relics of the church. After them came old men and fair young maidens. Last came the fighters, and with them were their wives and little children, and they all fell down before the king and begged for mercy.

Whether from policy or from kindness, William pardoned the repentant city, and forbade his soldiers to touch the property of the citizens. The only penalty that he demanded was an increase of tribute money and the destruction of two score of houses to make room for the castle which he intended to build. William marched on to the west through Devonshire and Cornwall. The land of those who rebelled was confiscated, and nearly all Cornwall, besides many rich manors of Devonshire and Somerset, was given to his brother Robert.

At last the king ventured to send for his queen. Once more his favorite "Mora" crossed the Channel, this time with a noble embassy, and returned with Matilda and a goodly company of knights and lords and ladies of the court. Some three centuries earlier, because of the crime of a wicked queen, it had been decreed that she who held the highest place in the land should be known as the king's wife, and not as the queen; but all this was forgotten, and Matilda was crowned at Westminster.

After the coronation there was a feast, and into the feasting hall came a newly appointed officer known as the "champion." Straight up and down the hall he rode, calling in a loud voice, "If any one denies that our most gracious sovereign lord William and his spouse Matilda are king and queen of England, he is a false-hearted traitor and a liar; and here I, as champion, do challenge him to single combat."

Several months later two thegns were talking of the coronation.

"No one ever heard before of a champion to prove that the king was king," said one.

"No one would ever dare to say that he was not king," said the other.

"Not without an army," said the first.

"It may be that some day we shall have a king who was born among us, even if he is not of our own people."

"Yes, after we and our children and our children's children are dead."

"Before then, perhaps. Have you not heard that in our own Yorkshire the queen has given birth to a son?"

"No," said the other; "is it true?"

"It is true, and something else is true, for the king says this boy shall be brought up as an Englishman, and shall learn to speak our language as well as that smooth, silly talk that they use at court."

"The king knows no English."

"True, but he says he will learn it."

"And so he would if it could be learned with a sword and a spear."

All of England south of the Thames was now under William's control, but there was trouble in the north. The northern earls, Edwin and Morcar, were at William's court, as was the boy Edgar. To Edgar, Morcar came one day and whispered:—

"Do you wish to be king?"

"Yes," said the boy.

"The north is free, and the north calls for you as its king. Will you go?" The boy agreed, and he and the two earls stole away from the court. Edwin had a special grievance because King William had promised him one of his daughters in marriage and had not yet been willing to give the earl his bride. William pursued, capturing one town after another on his way. The earls yielded, and Edgar fled with a third earl to Scotland.

Wherever William went, he conquered; and wherever he conquered, he distributed the forfeited land among his loyal subjects, generally Normans. All over the country rose the heavy, thick-walled castles with their square dungeon towers, saying ever to the helpless people, "Submit or be crushed."

On and on marched William. Nottingham yielded, and at York the trembling citizens hastened to meet him even before he had come near the walls of the city, and brought hostages and begged him to accept the keys of their city gates. How much against their will this was, is shown by the eagerness with which they admitted Edgar and his party only a few months later.

Now York was as important a town in the north as Exeter was in the south, and the king again hastened north and took a fearful revenge on the city. The story is that he would have marched on to Durham at break of day, but there was no break of day, for so heavy a darkness shut down upon the land that no man could see his neighbor. While the army stood in fear of what might happen, a voice chanted from out of the gloom:—

"Durham is the town of the holy Saint Cuthbert, and he it is who forbids you to harm his sacred city or even to enter it." It is just possible that William did not care to go any farther at that time, and had arranged the matter of the ghostly voice coming from the darkness, as he did once before when he wished to drive King Henry from Normandy. At any rate, he returned to London, but to a lonely palace, for the queen and the royal children had returned to Normandy, whose claims could be no longer neglected.

William might well have felt discouraged if he had known what the feeling was, for the sons of Harold came from Ireland and made an attempt to enter England from the west; and in the north the English were joyful over the coming of the Danes, whom they had been urging to join them as allies.

The boy Edgar and Waltheof, Earl of Northampton, were at the head of the army that now marched upon York. They captured the city and the Norman garrison; and if they had only been united, they might possibly have held the north against the king. As it was, they soon separated; it may be because of William's secret bribes to the Danes. Earl Waltheof yielded and paid homage to the king. William restored him to his estate and soon afterward gave him his niece Judith in marriage.

William had conquered the north, but the English who dwelt there might revolt at any moment, and at any moment the Humber might be filled with Danish ships. William's one purpose was to be master of England. Be the means harsh or gentle, he would be master. Never again should the north revolt. His favorite weapon was starvation rather than the sword. Starvation should meet every one who might venture to oppose his rule. He swept over the land like a flame of fire. To and fro, hither and thither, went the king and his men, leaving behind them ruined crops, smoking storehouses, and slaughtered animals. Property of every kind was burned. Pestilence came. Men sickened or starved, or became slaves to anyone that would give them a mouthful of food. Death was everywhere, but William had had his way, and never again did the north revolt.

And in York, the miserable, half-burned city, did the king of England determine to celebrate his Christmas. It should be kept with all ceremony, too, and the crown and the royal robes were brought to York, and within the walls of the half-ruined church, blackened by the fires of warfare, and with ruin and desolation and death on every side as far as the eye could see, the priests chanted the Christmas songs of gladness, and the king wore the crown which had been made sure by so fearful a sacrifice.

CHAPTER XV

A STERN RULE

T HE king was seated firmly on his throne. The south was submissive; the north was a wilderness. Far to the northwest was one last stronghold, the city of Chester, and William now set out to subdue it, and so complete the circle of his conquests. He was at York, and it was not long after Christmas, in a bitter northern winter; but William gave the order to march to Chester, and the army marched.

It was a terrible march. There were no roads. It was a wild, rough country at best, with streams, forests, valleys, and jagged hills, difficult in summer even for fresh, enthusiastic troops; but in the winter to make a way through valleys choked with snow, over hills bleak and slippery, and through forests that were masses of icy thorns and tangled icy boughs, would have been hard enough for men born and bred in the north. It was doubly hard for the soldiers from the sunny land of France, wearied by the previous campaigns, their first enthusiasm exhausted by this never satisfied commander, who was ever crying, "On, on," and it is no wonder that the murmurs grew louder and louder.

"I wish I was back in my own Anjou," said one soldier under his breath to a man from Brittany.

"Brittany isn't so bad a place," said the Breton. "We had enough to eat there, and here we may live on fogs and icicles or else starve."

"If any one denies that I, a man from Maine, am a good fighter, he is a false-hearted traitor and a liar," said a man from Maine, looking cautiously around him, and then strutting up and down in grotesque imitation of the "champion." Every one laughed, but one said:—

"There's as much earnest as fun in that, my friend from Maine; for not many men would have been willing to go up the scaling ladder first as you did at Exeter."

"Then if you will agree that I am not a coward, I will say that I don't want to fight any more of these English. They strike like demons."

"I'd as soon fight a demon as anything else," said the man of Anjou; "and I'd go up two scaling ladders to eat a good dinner in a comfortable hall with a red fire on the hearth and plenty of tapestry to keep the wind out." More and more did such feelings spread, till at last some one was found bold enough to say to the king:—

"King William, your soldiers would speak with you." Then the king went forth to his men, and one said, though not without some trembling:—

"King William, we are tired of hunger and cold and of this continual marching on and on. Your orders are too hard for men to carry out. Give us our dismissal." Not a moment did the king hesitate. He stood before them and said:—

"You who are faithful, follow me. You who are cowards, get you gone; it is nothing to me whether you follow or not." Now the soldiers could not make their way to France alone and without the resources of the king. They had hoped to make him turn back, or at least, to offer them higher wages, but the plan had failed. There was nothing to do but to follow him and by their bravery to try to make him forget their attempted desertion. They went on through forest and marsh, in the midst of snow and icy rain, and Chester was taken. The army marched south. On the plain of Sarum William reviewed his troops and rewarded them.

England was quiet, but it was not all peace and happiness through the land. There was discontent and bitter hatred and sometimes revolt, but William was king; and revolt was no longer against a man seeking power, but against a man holding power. William was never intentionally cruel. He had no wish to maim, to starve, to slaughter; but having set before him the single aim of subduing England, he would allow nothing to stand in his way. He would tear down a rebellious castle and put its defenders to the sword; but afterward, and almost without being asked, he would grant a free pardon to the man who had closed the castle gates against him.

Now that he was fairly settled in England, swarms of people came from the continent; for they looked upon England as a new country where, if a man was only a good soldier and vassal, he might receive broad stretches of land. Whole families came. An old rhyme says:—

> "William de Coningsby
> Came out of Brittany
> With his wife Tiffany
> And his maide Maufas
> And his dogge Hardigras."

William never despised the English. He tried to learn their language, encouraged marriages between English and Normans, and when he was not engaged in subduing his new people, he did all that he could to make them friendly with his old subjects. Unfortunately, many of the conqueror's army and of those that came after them were men of low birth, and the English despised them even while they yielded.

"These adventurers," said one English noble to another, "they are a rabble, and they follow a low-born king."

"There is no place here for an Englishman," said the other, "and I mean to take my own good sword and cut my way to the east. The emperor will always give an Englishman a welcome."

"So say I," said the other heartily. "My country is mine no longer; it belongs to these vagabonds. I will go to Denmark. The Danes were better friends to us than this great Norman with his haughty crew." So it was that while many people came to England, many left their country for foreign lands. Even if a man had sworn fealty to the king and was in his own house, he knew not when some wild band of marauders might come upon him,—against the king's will, of course, but the king was far away. It was better to defend one's goods than to try to restore them; and so the houses were filled with weapons, and the doors were barred and bolted.

Many hid themselves in the wide tracts of forests. Sometimes whole families with their servants, if they had any, went to the wild-wood. "The conqueror has stolen from us, why should we not take back what we can?" they said; and so they fell upon the Normans who came their way. The usual punishments did so little in preventing these assassinations that a law was made imposing a fine upon the people of every district in which a murdered man was found. To avoid this fine the English would, whenever a man was found dead, destroy his clothes and weapons, and then they would declare that the body was that of an Englishman. To meet this state of things, a law was made that every man found murdered should be regarded as a Frenchman unless two men and two women, all near relatives of the murdered man, should swear that he was English.

Although the conquered people never felt the least affection for William, they admitted that he was a just man, if he was severe; but for his companions they seem to have felt only scorn and hatred. They were willing to fight under the king, and especially if they could fight Frenchmen, for they looked upon all who spoke the French language as belonging to their oppressors. William had subdued English with French, and now he would subdue French with English, for Maine had revolted. Le Mans, which he had conquered ten years before, was determined to be free.

Matilda seems never to have made any long stay in England, for so long as William must be away from his duchy, so long must she and Robert stay in Normandy to rule over it. It was at their call that William crossed the Channel. He appeared before Le Mans with his army, and the conquest was only the old story repeated; for instead of fighting, he appealed to the men of Le Mans to surrender, that there might be no bloodshed. After one day's deliberation the town yielded, and William was as merciful as usual to his fallen foe.

The one instance in which he seems to have shown no mercy is in the case of the great Earl Waltheof, to whom he had given his niece Judith in marriage. It seems that Roger, son of the king's old friend, Fitz-Osbern, wished his sister to marry a Breton noble. For some reason the king forbade the marriage. Nevertheless, there was a great wedding, and many prominent men were present, both English and Normans, although they knew that it was against the king's will. Very bold were they in their speeches.

"He has stolen our land from us," said a Saxon.

"And we," said a Norman, "what have we received? We put him on a throne—the grandson of a tanner on a throne—and he has rewarded us with half-barren tracts of land. The land in Normandy is rich with vineyards and with grain fields. This reward of ours is rich in fogs and forests." Then arose another

Norman and turned to Earl Waltheof, who had sat silent, pouring the last drops of wine in his horn into another and then back again.

"Earl Waltheof," said he, "all that you English need is a man to lead. You are the man. If you and we two Normans unite, we can bring back the days of Edward. We need do no harm to the king, but we can prevent the oppressions of his nobles. Moreover, William is in Normandy, he is fighting, and he may never be able to return, and—"

"William not return?" said another Norman; "he has spent his life in battles and never yet has he received a wound. He'll return."

"Let him, when we are ready to receive him," said the first Norman. "There may be another Senlac, and if there is we will finish Battle Abbey, but it shall be in memory of William's defeat, not of his victory. We do not all love him any more than you do." Waltheof seemed to have heard not a word of this speech. At last he yielded against his will, and troops began to assemble.

"Do not hasten to cross the seas," wrote William's chief adviser to the absent king. "It would be a shame for you to have to come to us to drive out a handful of traitors and robbers." The royal forces met the conspirators and subdued them after one battle. Waltheof might have escaped, but trusting in his comparative innocence, he crossed the Channel, went straight to William, and begged for his forgiveness. Instead of receiving pardon, he was executed—the last of the English earls, and the only man executed, save for crime, in the whole of William's reign.

"And it was all his wicked wife," said an English thegn; "she wanted to get rid of her husband, and she told King William falsely that the earl had engaged a Danish fleet to come over to fight against him."

"King William made her marry Waltheof," said another; "she did not wish to be his wife."

"He was the best man in England," said the first.

"Perhaps she is sorry now. At any rate, it was she who besought the king to let the earl's body be taken from the hole between the cross-roads and buried at the convent of Croyland."

"She was afraid his spirit would trouble her," said the first, "and I don't wonder. The cousin of a friend of my wife's knows a man who has been at the convent, and he said that this Judith came there and brought a rich silken drapery, costly enough to be a prince's ransom, to throw over his tomb; but that whenever she tried to lay it down, an arm that no one could see would thrust it back as if a strong wind had blown it; and he says that at last she dropped the cloth on the ground and would never come near the tomb again."

And what had become of Edgar, heir to the English throne, last of the male line of the old royal family? For a long while he seemed to be at the call of any one that wanted to use him as a figurehead for a revolt. Apparently William had no special fear of him so long as he remained in England, or was visiting his sister who had married the king of Scotland; but, finally, King Philip of France, not so young as he was, but fully as pert, and as jealous of William as ever, invited Edgar to make his home in a French castle; then, although William did not interfere, he kept a close watch of the English prince.

Edgar set out for France in a finely decorated vessel laden with beautiful furs and many other rich presents from the Scotch king. If the vessel had been as seaworthy as it was handsome, the story might have had a different ending; but a great storm arose, and the ship was driven upon the coast of England. Without the load of gifts, Edgar and his men made their way back to Scotland as best they could.

"It is the will of God," said the Scotch king. "He has sent His storm that you may not resist the man whom He has chosen to rule. Do not fight against the decree of God, but send messengers to William and ask that there may be peace between you."

Edgar yielded, as he always did to whatever the last speaker advised. The messengers were sent, and King William replied with the utmost friendliness.

"I would gladly show all kindness," said William, "to him who is first of the English nobles." Then William sent an honorable embassy to bring Edgar to Normandy. Edgar was now the guest of a king, and he travelled in as much luxury as the times would permit. At every castle on the way a feast was made for him and his party. This time the sea was kind to him, and he came to the Norman court in safety. The king gave him one silver pound a day, and for many years he lived at the Norman court, satisfied with his silver pound, his dogs and horses, and the small manors which William allowed him in England.

There were three of William's deeds that especially aroused the wrath of the people,—the law of the curfew bell, the forming of the New Forest, and the compiling of the Doomsday Book. The curfew was a bell that rang at sunset in summer and at eight o'clock in winter, and when it struck, the fire on the hearth must be covered with ashes and the lights put out. This was an old regulation on the continent in order to prevent fires, and it was especially necessary in London, where there were only wooden houses; but it was new to the English, and though they were such early risers that few of them cared to sit up later or had lights good enough to make longer evenings a pleasure, they felt it a great act of tyranny to oblige them to blow out their candles at any fixed time.

The curfew law hurt their pride rather than did them any real injury; but they had a more serious grievance in the forming of the New Forest, as it was called, and as it has been called for eight hundred years. William had chosen Winchester, the favorite home of the Saxon kings, as his own dwelling place. It is north of the Isle of Wight, and easily approached from the sea. A little to the southwest of the city, and bordering on the shore, was a fertile tract of land containing some sixty thousand acres. It was partly wooded and partly open, and in the open places were homes of some of the English and some small settlements. These people were driven away to find an abode where they could, and their houses were torn down. More trees were planted, so as to make it as nearly like a wild country as possible.

No one knows just why William did this. It may have been in order to provide a place for the landing of his Norman forces that would be safe even in a time of general revolt. The deep forest would also be a good place for meetings of conspirators; and to prevent any dangers arising from such meetings there were most severe laws against carrying weapons into this region.

This is what some say, but others recall the fact that the one amusement that seemed to give the king any pleasure was hunting, and they believe that his only reason for making this tract of land into a desert was that he might have near his home a good field for his chosen sport.

Now among the earlier kings of England hunting had been as serious a business as repelling Danish invaders, and two hundred years before this time King Ethelwulf had feared lest some day England should be deserted and be given up to wild beasts. Only one hundred years before the coming of the Normans a certain Welsh prince was required to present every year a tribute of three hundred wolves' heads. Even in William's day, there were not only deer, but there were wolves and wild boars that must be killed for the safety of the flocks and herds. To destroy these would have been a praiseworthy deed; but to hunt merely for the pleasure of killing was not so common in England as in France, and many of the English looked upon William's enjoyment of the chase with a real horror. Whatever William's reasons were, the New Forest was made.

The desire of the poor people to remain in their old home was looked upon by the Normans much as the desire of a horse to remain in the same place and with the master whom he knows and loves is often looked upon to-day. To drive these people out from home to live or die as they might, seemed to the Normans as innocent a deed as it seems to some people of to-day to drop a petted kitten in a strange street and abandon it to its fate. Even those among the English who were well-to-do would not look upon these evictions of the poor people as nearly so much of a crime as was the severity of the laws against trespassing within the limits of the king's hunting ground. William "loved the wild animals as if he was their father," says the Anglo-Saxon Chronicle with a touch of grim irony, and he decreed terrible penalties for every trespass. The man that shot a deer must lose both his eyes—a punishment which generally resulted in death. People stood aghast and whispered:—

"The hand of God will be upon him. A curse rests upon his forest. That he might have idle sport, he has made men suffer, and suffering will surely come to him and to his."

The third deed of William which was especially objectionable to the English was the compilation of the Doomsday Book. The Danes had come many times, and might come again, and in any case it was necessary that the king should know what money he could collect for the expenses of the kingdom and for its protection. He had tried to levy a tax on land; but the value of land varied so widely in different places that the tax was not fairly apportioned, and so it was exceedingly hard to collect. There was another reason for the difficulty.

"You told us," said the Norman nobles, "that the land which we should win with our swords should be our own, and now you tax us to increase your own hoard." William replied:—

"You think of yourselves; I think of the country. You plan to raise flocks and cultivate the ground and make yourselves rich; I plan to strengthen the kingdom, lest some day an enemy fall upon us and we have not the means of defence."

Whether the holders of land were pleased or not, the survey did not stop. Commissioners were appointed to go all over England except in the northern districts, where the land had perhaps been little cultivated since the great devastation. They did their work thoroughly. "How much woodland, meadow, pasture, and ploughed land is there?" the commissioners asked. "How many people? How many cows, oxen, sheep, swine? How much did the manor bring in when King Edward reigned? How much when King William gave it? How much does it bring in now?"

The people, both English and Normans, were most indignant about this book. The curfew bell was not so serious a matter after all, and as for the New Forest, they could easily keep out of it; but this census was a different thing. The commissioners came to every house, and the people said:—

"It is a shame for a great king to send men to peer into the private affairs of his people. What is it to him whether we have a hive of bees or not?" Nevertheless, the survey went on, and the records were put into a great book and kept in the king's treasury at Winchester. The Normans called this book the *King's Roll*, or the *Winchester Roll;* but the Saxons named it indignantly the *Doomsday Book*, or the book of final decisions.

Early in the August of 1086, a remarkable meeting was held at Sarum. It was common on the continent for one man to pay homage to several persons. If dissensions arose between any two or three persons, it was sometimes a question with which one the vassal should stand. William meant to have no such trouble; and he called together his bishops, abbots, nobles, every man in the kingdom who held a piece of land, and required them to swear to obey him against all other men.

In 1066, England had one conqueror; in 1070, one king; in 1086, the land became one country.

CHAPTER XVI

THE LAST YEAR

IN all these years of trouble and anxiety, of false friends and bitter enemies, William's one joy had been the companionship of his wife and children,— when he could have them with him in England, or could be with them in Normandy. Matilda shared his ambition, and endured the frequent separation as patiently as might be, trying to rule the duchy in such wise that her husband might be free for the difficulties of England.

In the town of Bayeux, there is kept with the utmost care a piece of embroidery that Matilda and her court ladies are supposed to have wrought in William's honor during some of these absences. Embroidery was not looked upon in those days as a trivial amusement, it was a serious occupation; and it is quite possible that Matilda's excellent management of the turbulent duchy was not regarded with nearly so much respect and admiration as her skill in the use of the needle. Tapestry was not only the comfort that made life endurable in the draughty old castles; it was the family record, the history, the children's picture-book, and the grown folks' portrait gallery.

This Bayeux tapestry, as it is called, is a piece of canvas about half a yard wide and nearly seventy yards long. It is covered with figures of men and horses and trees and ships and castles,—hundreds of them; and these pictures, together with a running inscription in Latin, tell the whole story of the Norman conquest, beginning with Harold's visit to Normandy, and ending with the battle at Senlac. While the stone castles have crumbled, and the steel weapons of the fighters have vanished, this fragile piece of linen has endured for eight hundred years. The care with which it is wrought suggests that it was a labor of love; and it seems a great pity that between the man who did such bold deeds and the woman who loved to chronicle them, dissension should have arisen. Dissension did arise, however, and it was on account of the one who was dearest to them both,—their eldest son, Robert.

William had always been troubled lest the barons should revolt at his death and refuse their allegiance to his son. It was because of this fear that before he went to England he required all his vassals to do homage to Robert, who was then twelve years of age; and to make the matter even more sure, he called upon the king of France, as overlord, to confirm this transaction. Whenever William was in England, Robert's name was associated with his mother's in the government of the duchy, until, while he was yet a boy, he began to feel like a very great man; and when he was about twenty-three, he demanded that his father's domain should be limited to England, and that he himself should have the full control of Normandy.

"I don't take off my clothes till I go to bed," said the conqueror. "Normandy is mine because I inherited it, and England is mine because I won it; but if I gave up Normandy, I could not hold England."

"What am I to do, then?" asked Robert angrily. "How am I to pay my followers?"

"Obey me," said William, "and wherever I have power, there shall you have power; wherever I have wealth, there shall you have wealth."

"I won't be the hireling of any man," said Robert; "I want what belongs to me. You give me Normandy, and then you take it away. Normandy belongs to me, and I want it."

"A son who does not know how to obey his father is not fit to rule a duchy," said William. "Go to Canterbury and ask Archbishop Lanfranc how a son should behave toward his father before you come to me for a duchy."

"My lord the king," said Robert, "I did not come here to listen to lectures; I had enough of that from my tutors when I was a boy. I came for the duchy of Normandy, which is mine by right. Will you give it to me, or will you not?"

"I will *not*," thundered the king. "So long as I live, what is mine is mine."

Robert went away in a rage. The more he thought of the matter, the more angry he grew, and the more ready to listen to his companions and to the messages of Philip of France that were ever urging him on to demand his rights. The younger sons, William

"A SON WHO DOES NOT KNOW HOW TO OBEY
HIS FATHER IS NOT FIT TO RULE A DUCHY,"
SAID WILLIAM

Rufus and Henry, held by their father, and Robert's jealousy of them made him ready to quarrel on the slightest pretext.

It soon came about that William went forth to quell a Norman revolt, and his three sons accompanied him, though Henry could hardly have been more than nine or ten years old. The little boy and William Rufus were playing at dice in the room directly over Robert, and either in malice or in mischief, they threw water down upon their brother and his friends below. Robert chose to regard the silly trick as a deliberate insult, and rushed upstairs with his drawn sword to take a fearful revenge. Fortunately, the king appeared and prevented violence, but that very night Robert and a company of his friends rode to Rouen and made an attempt to seize the castle. This was unsuccessful; and Robert then declared that he would stay no longer in a duchy which was his own and was unjustly kept from him by another; so out into the world he went, visiting wealthy knights and nobles, and arousing them against his father by telling them how unjustly he had been treated. There were many in Normandy who, in spite of their oath to William, would provide Robert with money on his promise to repay them liberally when he should come to his rights; and Philip of France was always ready to do anything that would work to the injury of William.

Robert had yet another grievance; and that was that when he was a child his father had betrothed him to the little girl who was the heiress of Maine, on condition that the revenues of Maine were to belong to William till the children were old enough to be married. The little girl died; and as there was no one else who had a good title to the district, William kept it; and when Robert demanded it as his right, declared that there had been no marriage, and therefore Robert had no claim to the province.

King William's love for his children was as strong as his manifestation of it was often unwise, and this rebellion would have been enough to make him unhappy; but worst of all, he found after a while that Matilda was secretly supporting Robert's rebellious plans by sending him the money that was increasing and arming the foes of her husband. Again and again he forbade it. The proud queen pleaded for her son. Then said the king:—

"Could you have found a husband who would have loved you more than I, or have been more faithful to you? Where I am duke, you are duchess; where I am king, you are queen. My treasures are in your hand. Can it be that you are pouring them out to aid my enemy, that you whom I have loved best of all the world are the one that has betrayed me?" And Matilda answered:—

"You have shared with me all that you have because you love me; and can you blame me that I share with Robert all that I have because I love him? If he was dead and buried in the earth seven feet deep, I would give my own heart's blood to bring him to life again. I cannot be so hard-hearted as to abandon my eldest son, and you must not lay such a command upon me." Then William declared that at least her messenger should be punished; but Matilda sent word to the man, and he fled to a convent, "and so saved at the same time his body and his soul," say the old chroniclers.

Finally, there was a pitched battle between father and son and their followers. An arrow shot down the king's horse, and at the same moment William, who in all his battles had never before received a wound, was pierced through the arm by a spear thrust. It was Robert who bore the spear, and upon him his father pronounced a bitter curse. Afterwards, by the entreaties of the queen and the chief men of the duchy, a kind of reconciliation was brought about; but the thought that his queen was no longer one with him, and that to please a prodigal son she would aid his enemies, was perhaps the greatest grief of the king's whole life.

One sorrow after another came to him. Not long after Robert's rebellion, a messenger stood before him with pale face and downcast eyes.

"O King William," he said, "the prince was pursuing a deer in the New Forest, and his horse took fright and dashed him against a tree, and he is dead." Prince Richard was buried in the church at Winchester. After the funeral a little group of English lingered about the place.

"It is not easy to lose a son," said one.

"No, it is not," said an old man. "My son was killed at Senlac. If William had stayed in the land that God gave him, his son would not have been killed and neither would mine."

"They say that the prince fell from his horse just where the altar of the church used to stand," said the first.

"So I have heard," said the old man; "and I have also heard that every night as the curfew rings, the dead priests come out in white robes and walk around the place where their church used to be. One of them bears the golden pyx, and in it is the semblance of the Holy Wafer, and as they go, they chant, 'There shall be three, there shall be three.' This is the first; who will be the second?"

"Perhaps the king himself," whispered the other fearfully. "Since the murder of Waltheof nothing has gone well with him. Then, too, he married against the will of the church, and it is only right that one should die and one rebel. When a man does wrong, he is sure to suffer."

William's other two sons had stood by their father. Of his daughters, the little girl who had been promised to Harold had never crossed the water, for she died before the conquest. Cicely entered a convent, as did also a younger sister. One married the Count of Brittany, and another, the Count of Blois.

A fine trait in William's character was his affection for his relatives on the side of his peasant mother. Of Arletta herself nothing is known, except that she married an honorable knight, Herlwin de Conteville, and that William always treated her with great respect. Her two sons, Robert and Odo, had stood one on either side of William at the battle of Senlac. Robert was a brave, true, upright man, and he seems to have been one of the few whom William dared to trust; for while in giving land to other men, he was careful to scatter their manors about the kingdom, to Robert he gave nearly the whole of Cornwall and seventy-five manors in Devonshire, besides nearly five hundred more in different parts of the country. Robert fought not only with William, but for him, and was never tempted to have the least connection with the endless conspiracies that were made against his royal brother.

Odo, the second son of Arletta, was of quite different material. He had been raised to the bishopric of Bayeux; but he was more of a warrior than a bishop, and he gladly dropped his staff and seized a war-club when the opportunity came to him to win great possessions in England. William made him Earl of Kent, and gave him a great number of manors; but not nearly so many as he gave Robert, and far more scattered.

When William had to leave England for Normandy, the chief rule of the country was given to Odo, as has been said before. Wealth and power coming to him so suddenly were more than he could bear with wisdom. He began to think of aiming at the royal throne. Then some evil counsellor whispered to him:—

"There is a soothsayer in Rome who says that the name of the next pope will be either Odo or Otto."

"It shall be Odo," said the bishop to himself; and from that moment he was like one insane in his ambition to become pope. He bought himself a beautiful house in Rome; he sent munificent gifts to all whose influence might be of value; and he even planned to enter the holy city with so large an escort that it was almost like an army. But William had not been blind; and just when Odo was ready to set sail with his company, who should appear on the scene but the king of England. He straightway called an assembly of the chief men, and to them he said:—

"Here is the man who has ruled England in my name, while I was quelling a revolt in my duchy and suppressing the rebellion of my unnatural son. He has robbed the poor and the church. He has planned to seize the popedom as he has seized the goods of my subjects. My knights who are needed in England he has persuaded to abandon their own country to the Danish hosts or to any marauders that may come, while they themselves guard his way to Rome that he may become pope. Here is the man. What is fitting to be done with him?" No one wished to speak. There was silence. Then said the king:—

"No man who has done ill should be spared through favor. Seize this man and put him in ward." No one dared to seize a bishop. Thereupon William himself laid hold of him.

"I am a priest," cried Odo, "a minister of the Lord. No one may condemn a bishop without the decree of the Pope."

"A bishop?" said William. "I have nothing to do with a bishop. The bishop may go where he will. The one I have to do with is the Earl of Kent, he who has ill-treated my people, he who is my vassal and my earl." Then was the Earl of Kent carried away and put into prison. The Pope was indignant, but William replied only:—

"Naught have I to do with the bishop, he may go free; but the earl remains in prison."

Only one year after the trouble with Odo, the king was suddenly called to Normandy by the fatal illness of Matilda. He had met his other troubles bravely; but her loss was a crushing blow, and one from which he never recovered.

Four years after the death of Matilda came the last year of William's life. It was a terrible time. There were disastrous fires in many of the chief towns of England, and the land was ravaged by fearful storms. Then came famine, and after famine came sickness. With all this there was war as fierce as any that had been fought during the whole reign.

A strip of territory called the Vexin had been given by France to Duke Robert, then seized again by France when William was a child. William demanded this land of Philip, but Philip, knowing that the king was not at all well, ventured to return no other reply than a coarse, impertinent jest. In a moment there flashed through William's mind the wrongs that he had endured from Philip's father, the insolence of Philip himself, and worst of all, the eager encouragement to rebellion that Philip had given to his son Robert. He sprang from his bed, assembled his troops, and whirled over the Vexin like a storm-wind, laying waste homes and harvest-fields. At last he came to Mantes; and there palace and church blazed alike, till the ground where the town had stood was only a bed of glowing embers. On one of these the horse of William stumbled. The king fell forward heavily upon the pommel of the saddle. He felt that his injury was mortal and sounded a retreat. He was taken to Rouen, and thence to the quiet priory of Saint Gervase on a hill to the west of the city.

About him gathered bishops and abbots and men skilled in medicine. There, too, came his faithful brother Robert; and his two younger sons, William Rufus and Henry, who waited eagerly for the suffering man to declare his final will in regard to his property.

"Who shall have Normandy?" they questioned.

"Normandy was promised to Robert," said the king. "Ill fares the land that he rules, but the Normans have done him homage; they wish for him, and Normandy he must have."

"And who is to have England?" cried William Rufus, with sparkling eyes; but his face fell when his father said slowly:—

"Normandy is mine as it was my father's, but England I took by the sword. I give it back to God; the land is not mine to bestow." His eyes closed wearily, and William Rufus turned bitterly away.

"My lord king," said one of the bishops, "is it well to leave the country to the strife and tumult that befall the land that has no ruler? Will you not name him to whom you would give your kingdom?"

"It is not mine to give," said the king; "but if it was mine, I would give it to my son William. Yes, write a parchment to Lanfranc. Tell him my son has been obedient to me, and that if it please God, I would that he should have the kingdom. Tell Lanfranc to crown him if he thinks it right." The parchment was prepared, and William sealed it with his ring. Henry had been waiting impatiently. Now he broke forth:— ·

"And what am I to have, if Robert has the duchy and William the kingdom? What is there left for me?"

"I give you five thousand pounds in silver," said the king.

"What can I do with that," said Henry, "if I have no place to dwell in?"

"Be patient," said his father. "You are young; let those who are older go before you. The time may come when you will be greater than both of them."

The two young men left their father's bedside: Henry to have his silver weighed and to put it into a place of safety; William Rufus to set out for England, lest some one seize the throne before him. Then William gave large sums of money to rebuild Mantes, to aid the church, and to help the poor of England. He named over one prisoner after another, and bade that they be released.

"There is one more," said an abbot; "there is Bishop Odo. Will you not set him free?"

"No," said the king; "bishop and brother I would gladly free, but the earl who has plundered and oppressed my people, he shall not go free. Open every other prison door in Normandy and in England, but bar his more firmly." Then said Robert of Mortain, Earl of Cornwall:—

"He is our brother, William, our own mother's son. Set him free, and I pledge all that you have given me that he will no longer oppress those who cannot resist. By your love for me, by your love for our mother, set him free."

"Ruin and woe will follow him wherever he goes," said William; "but as you will. Set him free."

One September morning a few days later the great bell on the church struck.

"What is that?" asked William.

"It is the bell for primes," said the attendant. William clasped his hands, and with a prayer for pardon his spirit passed away. The Anglo-Saxon Chronicle says:—

"May Almighty God show mercy to his soul, and grant his sins forgiveness."

As to William's greatness, there is no question. More than one man of resolute purpose has cut for himself a way to a throne with his own good sword, and that, indeed, is an achievement; but it is a greater when one placed at the head of a turbulent, rebellious state has reduced that state to order, and has extended his sway over a rich and powerful kingdom. Here is a man who began his reign as a little child, envied because of his princely father and despised because of his plebeian mother. Whoever chose might cast a glance of scorn at the boy of ignoble birth. Whoever aspired to a duchy might attempt his murder. Other children grew up amid love; he grew up amid hatred. Could one expect such a childhood to bring forth tenderness, gentleness, and mercy? Could one ask more than that those years should not make him bitter and malevolent?

And yet this child proved to be a man of warmest affections. He clung to his low-born mother. To her he presented the first-fruits of his sword; to her son, of all the nobles that stood by him at Senlac, he gave the largest share of the conquered kingdom. He showed a savage cruelty more than once, it is true, but either to those who had taunted his mother, or to the king who had led astray his eldest son. Over and over again he forgave men who had revolted against him.

An eleventh-century man should not be judged by twentieth-century ideas. The standard of goodness is higher, and the moral man of William's time would be looked upon to-day as a dangerous character. What was then the simple course of justice would be to-day the most barbaric cruelty. It was a time of formalism. He who committed no great crime, performed the penances of the church, and gave to her freely, was looked upon as her faithful son. To take a false oath one's self was generally regarded as wrong under most circumstances, but to trick another into a sacred promise was a different matter. Hildebrand had come none too soon. Morality was low; the demands of the church were low. If William seized England wrongfully, he was at least fighting under the Pope's banner, and with the blessing of the Pope resting upon his head.

Alfred the Great might well say, "I have sought to live my life worthily;" William the Conqueror could say, "I have given freely to the church; I have built many convents and many abbeys." Alfred was true to the spirit of the teachings of the church; William was true to the letter.